SCRAMBLE

LEVEL

SCRAMBLE

© 2018 by Marty Neumeier

All rights reserved

No part of this book may be reproduced or transmitted in any form or by any means, whether mechanical, photocopying, electronic, recording, or otherwise, without prior written permission from the publisher, except by a reviewer who may quote brief passages in a review

To report errors or request permissions, contact publisher@levelcmedia.com

www.martyneumeier.com

Publisher: Level C Media
Design production: Jameson Spence
Cover design: Marty Neumeier
Editing: Zach Gajewski

ISBN 978-0-9974102-7-3

SCRAMBLE

A BUSINESS THRILLER BY **MARTY NEUMEIER**

To Eileen

Books by Marty Neumeier

THE BRAND GAP (2003)
*How to bridge the distance between
business strategy and design*

ZAG (2006)
*The #1 discipline of high-
performance brands*

THE DESIGNFUL COMPANY (2009)
*How to build a culture of
nonstop innovation*

METASKILLS (2012)
Five talents for the Robotic Age

THE 46 RULES OF GENIUS (2014)
An innovator's guide to creativity

THE BRAND FLIP (2016)
*Why customers now run companies—
and how to profit from it*

BRAND A–Z (2017)
*An interactive dictionary
of 1,000 essential brand terms*

SCRAMBLE (2018)
*How agile strategy can build
epic brands in record time*

CONTENTS

	PREFACE	IX
1	SOKRATES	1
2	BIG SKY	5
3	HEADWINDS	10
4	REFLECTION	15
5	STRATEGY	19
6	TEAMWORK	24
7	NAYSAYERS	30
8	TRUST	34
9	KRYPTONITE	39
10	CIRCLES	44
11	MAYDAY	51
12	CHOICES	55
13	FIVE Qs	58
14	TRIBE	66
15	BATTLEGROUND	73
16	FIVE Ps	80
17	PINBALL	85
18	COOPERSTOWN	91
19	EPIPHANY	94
20	PROBING	100
21	ONLYNESS	111
22	CHECKPOINT	117
23	BLIZZARD	124
24	CHRISTMAS EVE	130
25	GIFTS	136
26	ANXIETY	142
27	JONAH	147
28	SWARMING	152
29	MISSION	158
30	TOUCHPOINTS	164
31	FIREWORKS	169
32	SCRAMBLE	176
33	BUILD-OUT	181
34	BULLETPROOFING	189
35	WIND-UP	195
36	PITCH	204
37	AFTERMATH	216
	AGILE STRATEGY	222
	THANKS	241
	THE AUTHOR	244

PREFACE

An audience of fifty executives leaned forward, listening intently. I'd been invited to speak on the topic of leadership and creativity. My message was simple: in a time of accelerating change, leaders can no longer *decide* the way forward; instead, they have to *design* the way forward. Customers want more than products and services. They want meaning. Personal growth. A chance to reach their full potential.

"We're not human beings," I said in closing, "we're human *becomings*."

The audience rose to its feet in heartfelt applause. I knew I'd nailed it. When the clapping subsided and everyone sat down, a hand shot up. An usher hurried over with a microphone. A forty-ish woman with flecks of gray in her hair stood up to speak.

"I think I understand what you're saying: leaders need to be more creative today," she said, consulting her notes. "We can't rely on old case studies for answers to new questions. We need to think about *what could be*, not just *what is* or *what has been*. The real innovation is the customer, not the product. We need to align our culture with the larger goals of customers."

She looked up. "These seem like good tips. And the tools you gave us are easy to understand. But I'm having trouble squaring the tools with my experience. I'm not sure how they'd feel in my hands. Do you know what I mean?"

Heads nodded vigorously around the room. I realized then that I *hadn't* nailed it. I attempted a response, but it sounded glib. I secretly thought, well, jeez, that's why you hire a company like ours. Did you really think you could learn everything from a talk? Yet I wanted to offer more than a sales pitch.

There's a famous saying among authors: all books are failures. That's because it's extremely difficult to transfer knowledge or experience from one person to another. Nowhere is this truer than with business books. They tend to be tedious, humorless, headache-inducing, repetitive, and long. They promise a miracle at twenty-five dollars, but die on the nightstand with a bookmark stuck in chapter one.

Ever since I gave that talk, the question of "how the tools would actually feel in my hands" has haunted me.

A CEO friend of mine got me thinking. He said, "What people really want is a realistic picture of how a new approach will work in their lives. Most business books are boring: they're full of case studies, abstract principles, and disembodied tools. They leave out the *experience* of adopting a new approach: the emotions, the obstacles, the setbacks, the human interaction, the relentless pressure. They don't give you a *feel* for the tools. Couldn't you just skip the case studies and tell a story?"

Thus was born *Scramble*, a fictional account of a young CEO in trouble. He and his team have five weeks to reimagine their company. If the board approves their plan, they'll live to fight another day. If not, they'll lose their jobs, their company, and everything they've been working for.

The tools at the heart of the book are the *five Qs* of strategy and the *five Ps* of design thinking. These make up the basic principles of *agile strategy*—a faster, more collaborative approach to trans-

Preface

forming a business. Agile strategy isn't rocket s[...] monsense approach that anyone can use for a [...] ness and organizational challenges.

Scramble is not only for leaders but for everyone in[...] building a business or brand. Whether you're a strategist, ma[...]keter, designer, writer, researcher, project manager, accountant, consultant, instructor, or venture capitalist, you'll find familiar challenges and recognizable faces in the book.

You'll also discover the ability to see your business in a new light—not as a static set of requirements, but as a living opportunity, a *becoming* that responds to passionate purpose and focused creativity.

At the back of the book I've included a "Guide to Agile Strategy," a recap of the principles highlighted in the story. You can download a copy of the guide and other useful tools from my website, martyneumeier.com.

If you enjoy *Scramble,* please share it with the people you work with. Agile strategy functions best when every member of the team has "a feel for the tools."

—*Marty Neumeier*

1

SOKRATES

Wednesday, December 1. The drizzle turned to rain, kicking up tiny spikes of water on the oily streets. David Stone pulled the handle of the Uber and piled into the back, slamming the door behind him. He flicked the button on his smartphone: *7:15 p.m.*

A pair of heavy eyebrows rose up in the rearview mirror. "Easy on the Prius," said the driver.

David apologized, still out of breath from his dash to the car.

"Hell's Kitchen?" said the eyes in the mirror.

"Right," said David, making a conscious effort to slow his breathing. "BigSky headquarters. Across from the Bull Building."

"Okaaay," said the driver. He swung the car in a sharp arc and pointed uptown. Angry horns blared from behind. The rain was quickening, and the windshield wipers beat frantically to keep up.

David's superior, Andy Vineyard, had sounded strange on the phone. Brusque. Impatient. Why call David back to the office at this hour? What was so important that it couldn't wait for morning?

True, things hadn't been going well. Revenues were down. The company's valuation had slipped since David had taken the reins in January. There were headwinds, factors far beyond his control. The economy was faltering. People weren't traveling as much. The country had turned inward. But he was doing his best; even Andy had said so. The two enjoyed a warm relationship: Andy, the avuncular mentor, and David, the promising young protégé. He'd never have taken the top job at BigSky without the steady support of its well-regarded founder.

"Excuse me for asking," said the driver. "You in some kind of trouble?" The eyes in the mirror again. "You look, uh, distressed."

"Drive," said David, falling back in his seat. He was allergic to talkative drivers, and this one looked like a real Chatty Cathy.

"Just so you know, there's a demonstration at the Bull Building. Streets are blocked off."

"Get me as close as you can," David said curtly. He checked his phone: *7:25*. He told Andy he'd be there by 7:40. Punctuality was hardwired in David.

Ever since last year, when Richard Bull won the presidency, the scene around the Bull Building had become one of constant chaos. Police cordoned off the nearby streets whenever Bull was back in town, and flash-mob protests erupted in front of the building every time he made one of his ill-considered pronouncements. It was an unkind trick of fate that BigSky was located directly across the street.

"I recognized you right away," said the driver, looking in the mirror. "CEO of the hotel company, right? Tough gig."

David considered whether to reply. Talk about a tough gig. This guy's an Uber driver. He doesn't realize he'll be booted out by bots in five years. He's wasting his life on a career with obsolescence baked into it. But David decided to bite. "What do you know about BigSky?"

"I know the stock price is down 30 percent from last year. And I know the financial press is out to get you."

"Oh really?"

"Yeah, and unless you do something soon you'll have picketers with pitchforks at your next shareholder meeting. Is that about right?"

David admitted it might be.

"Tell me. I'm just an Uber driver. Why can't you take some of your cash and do an end run?"

"What do you mean *end run*?" David could feel his patience fraying. He checked his phone: *7:40*. He was now officially late for the meeting.

"I mean, why can't you just build a new business and let the others simmer for a while? It's not like you can fix the economy."

David noticed a tattoo of questionable provenance poking out from underneath the driver's collar—it seemed like everybody was an armchair CEO these days. "Since when do Uber drivers follow the business news?"

"I won't be an Uber driver forever. I'm working on my executive MBA."

David had to chuckle inwardly. Never jump to conclusions. The world is rarely what it seems. After all, no one would have pegged David for a business guy in the early days, but here he was. "Where you going to school?"

The driver looked back. He was David's age, with dark features and a crooked smile. "Mostly right here," he said, gesturing toward the back seat. "You can't believe the people I get in my car."

"What people?"

"You know. People like you. Regulars."

"I thought Uber drivers had to pick up whoever's in the area. How can you have regulars?"

"Let's just say I got a dispensation from the pope." His smile widened. "Like I said, you can't believe the people I get in my car."

"You're not going to give me any names?"

"They're my advisory group, very private people. If I threw their names around, how would I get people like you to be regulars?"

"I'm not a regular."

"Not yet, but I have a feeling we're going to be good friends." He handed back a business card with the name *Dmitri Sokouris* on it. There was a phone number below the name. "My regs call me

Sokrates. With a *K*."

"Sokrates."

"Because I ask too many questions," he said with a diagonal smile. "Text me when you need a ride. I'll be there for you."

He pulled the car to the curb about a block from BigSky headquarters. The streets teemed with protesters, an angry crowd bristling with signs and staccato chants. Police stood by in riot gear.

David climbed out of the car onto the slippery sidewalk. Sokrates handed an umbrella through the window. "Take this. I'll get it back the next time I see you. Text me."

"What if I lose the card?" said David.

"It's not like I don't know where you live."

David shut the car door—more carefully this time—and covered the hundred yards to his office at a trot, dodging police and protesters like a quarterback unable to find a receiver. When he reached the doors of the BigSky lobby, they were locked. He fished for his keycard and let himself in.

Andy sat behind the big oak desk he'd bought when he started the business some forty years ago. Everyone else was gone for the day except the maintenance man, whose blurred silhouette was visible through the frosted glass of the next office, moving back and forth to the muffled sounds of an industrial vacuum. David apologized for his lateness. Andy waved it off. He pointed to a chair.

"Listen, David," he said. "I didn't want to do this by phone." His brow furrowed as he chose his words.

"I just met with the board. A couple of the members are getting antsy—you can probably guess which ones. I know we're not in danger yet, but the trend doesn't look good. At the rate we're going we could burn through our cash in about eighteen months, maybe sooner. Up until now we've had a remarkable run. But our shareholders are beginning to wonder if they'll ever see a payout. If you don't do something soon, the board will take matters into its own hands."

David was dumbfounded. He knew his progress was less than impressive—okay, a lot less—but he never expected anything like this. "Are you saying I'll be out?"

"I'm saying this is something only you can fix. You're the CEO. We're giving you five weeks to develop a turnaround strategy. If it looks reasonable, we'll find a way to fund it. If not, well…"

"I'm out. I get it. But *five weeks*? It takes most companies a good six to twelve months to design and vet a new strategy. Only five weeks? And over the holidays? How?"

"You figure it out," said Andy. "That's the deal. Frankly, I'm not sure how I'd do it myself. This is on you. Your moment of truth."

2

BIG SKY

Thursday, December 2. David couldn't sleep that night. He got to work early and holed up in his office with a pot of coffee. Pads of paper and a printed calendar lay on a wide, polished plank of reclaimed ash, a makeshift desk supported by two steel sawhorses. He sat staring through the window toward the Bull Building across the street.

Deep breath. Okay, five weeks equals thirty-five days. Subtract the week they were closed for the holidays, and that leaves a month—twenty-eight days to figure out this whole thing. He shook his head. What genius came up with this deadline? The annual meeting was scheduled for mid-January. Maybe the board wanted time to prepare a statement about his ouster if it didn't work out. He made a note to cancel his trip back home over Christmas. Realistically, he'd have to work straight through the holidays.

This is on you. David reasoned there was no benefit in pulling the other leaders off line, especially during a revenue crisis. He could bring them in when he had something concrete to talk about. He grabbed a yellow pad and jotted down a quick recap of the company's history:

> *1974—founded with 1 hotel—BigSky Nature Lodge— Bozeman, Montana—1st eco-lodge in US—photography, nature walks, eco-classes, tours of Yellowstone*
>
> *1979—Andy builds second hotel in Taos, New Mexico— wins awards for eco-friendly siting and building materials— called "architecturally significant" by Abitare magazine*
>
> *1988—company grows to 9 properties—incl. hotels in Big Sur, Badlands, Everglades—hotels win numerous awards— Andrew Vineyard on cover of Forbes, Businessweek*
>
> *1997—BigSky moves from Bozeman to NYC—replicates US formula in Latin America—Oaxaca, Mexico; Antigua, Guatemala; Machu Picchu, Peru; Iguazu Falls, Argentina; Patagonia, Chile; also in Hawaii—Waimea Canyon, Kauai; Kilauea, Hawaii*

David stared at his notes. The company's success was built on the simple insight that people had been hungry for a new kind of lodge experience. Not the traditional hunting, fishing, snowmobiling, motorbiking experience, but a more nuanced, nurturing one. Its offer was straightforward—a four-star experience at a three-star price. It didn't sound like much in the beginning, but it had proved sufficient. By 2003, the number of BigSky lodges had grown to nineteen.

In 2004, when Homeland Security forced the TSA to impose tougher airport screening, Andy became captivated by the concept of layover hotels. He calculated that a chain of low-cost airport hotels could not only pay for itself, but also fund a faster expansion of the eco-lodges.

He approached the architects at Sestina Partners, where David was CEO. They'd already completed several lodges for BigSky that had won awards and attracted new travelers.

"Here's my vision," he said to the architectural team. "A chain of airport hotels—I'm not sure what to call them—that combines high design and low prices. I have no preconceptions—just a hunch that people would like a cheaper place to stay. Travelers need a quick fix for all those mismatched schedules and missed connections. They could use a break."

The partners at Sestina grabbed that blank slate with both hands. David personally led the project. He and his team quickly discovered that the key to low cost—unsurprisingly—was a small footprint.

They researched compact living spaces: Japanese capsule hotels, tiny apartments, Pullman cars, luxury yachts.

They did their math. How much would it cost to clean a room? How much space do people need to feel comfortable? What new building methods could be used to slash construction costs?

They did their anthropology. What are travelers trying to accomplish? How could interior design lessen guests' claustrophobia? How could they keep low price from translating to low status?

They did their eco-planning. How could they save on the costs of heating, cooling, lighting, soundproofing, and elevators? How could they reduce waste from laundry, food, and bathrooms? How could they optimize space with a smarter hotel configuration?

The result was Sojourner—a radical new concept in layover hotels. Sojourner hotels were designed so they could easily be built, maintained, and managed. The rooms were modular and manufactured in local factories. A crew could snap together 128 rooms like Legos within a few weeks.

A heating and cooling system and a single elevator shaft were combined in a central core, drawing energy from sustainable sources. Geothermal ground loops powered the heating and cooling system; transparent voltaic cells on the exterior walls generated electricity.

The buildings' floor plans looked like starfish with three, four, or five legs, depending on the site and the size of the airport a specific hotel served. It took a staff of only two managers, four cleaners, an engineer, and two drivers to manage an average-sized property.

The rooms themselves were only six by twelve feet, and they were so efficient they could be cleaned in a quarter of the normal time. The bedding could be washed at half the normal cost. The rooms were arranged along double-loaded hallways that maximized space while letting in huge amounts of light from outside. Hallway length was limited to eight rooms per side, which obviated the need for staircases on each end.

And the experience?

When guests unlocked their rooms with their smartphones, they were greeted by a view of trees, not cars, through large, operable windows. Two CozyCots folded down from opposite walls to meet in the middle of the room, offering the option of a single or double bed. A hidden array of miniature speakers produced rich, ambient audio—guests could choose from a menu of calming natural sounds or pastoral music. The vaulted ceiling was a *trompe l'oeil* sky that artificially darkened from day to dusk to night, finally becoming a field of stars. Storage walls in the bathrooms were masterpieces of efficiency. An unenclosed shower captured extra space from the surrounding area.

All these innovations were delivered with the elegant design of a modern five-star hotel. But it was the price that knocked people out—$48 per night for one person, $68 for two.

The hospitality industry sat up. Pundits called the new properties *gotels*—hotels for people on the go. Andy was once again the darling of the business press. This time he generously shared the credit with Sestina.

When the dust had settled and the expansion was well underway, Andy invited David to dinner at Cosme, his favorite haunt in the Flatiron District.

"David," Andy said, refilling their glasses with a crisp Ambar chardonnay from Mexico, "you're an architect by training. A great one, in my opinion. You worked nights and weekends to get your MBA from NYU so you could lead Sestina to the top of your field…"

"Andy, it was a team—"

Andy held up his hand. "I know. It's always a team effort. Listen, David, have you ever considered leading a team for a larger company?"

"What size team and what kind of company?" David asked.

"The whole team at BigSky, all 3,500."

David was speechless. Ever since college he'd wanted to be an architect. He'd only tackled the business side of Sestina in self-defense. Architects aren't known for their business acuity, and if Sestina were ever to maximize its superior talent, someone had to step up to the plate. The firm needed to focus on work in its wheelhouse instead of swinging at every pitch. At first it felt strange. Eventually, however, David grew more confident in the leadership role. But a company with 3,500 employees and more than $400 million in revenues—that was a different story.

Andy continued. "Look, I'm getting up there. I'm nearing eighty now, and you're, what, mid-thirties? You've got a long runway in front of you. Mine is getting shorter by the day. I'm ready to step back from the operational details and take it easy. The chairmanship suits me fine. I just need a good pilot. What about it?"

David realized his mouth had fallen open. No words were coming out.

"Okay, I know it's a stretch. But I can show you the ropes. Think of the amazing things you'll build. I know you can handle it. What do you say?"

To David's surprise, he managed a yes. The next day he made his peace with his colleagues at Sestina, promising to send more projects as he was able.

But "handle it"? Here he was, after little more than a year on the job, staring out the window with no clue at all how to handle it. He'd already used every weapon in the arsenal. He mounted ad campaigns. Created special events. Forged strategic alliances. Remodeled older properties. Shuffled the org chart. He finally began laying off employees. Nothing moved the needle. His business-school case studies were no match for the economic headwinds blowing from the direction of the Bull Building.

3

HEADWINDS

Friday, December 3. He sat at the breakfast bar in his light-filled West Chelsea apartment. The *New York Times* lay spread out in front of him, open to the "Opinion" section. A half-eaten bagel and a cold cup of coffee sat next to the paper. He normally preferred reading the news on his tablet, but he still liked to luxuriate in the scent of fresh ink on crisp newsprint. He would use the tablet later to catch up with the *Wall Street Journal*.

He reached to the end of the bar for a pen, and then carefully underlined a passage from a column by Roger Cohen: *The world is not as it was. Beneath the Magic Mountain grim tides gather. Old assumptions seem obsolete. Apprehension is in the air.*

Apprehension indeed. Richard Bull insisted that the country was under threat of imminent attack—from immigrants, terrorists, journalists, even scientists. People were no longer safe in their homes, he implied, and even less so in another country. Circle the wagons. Pull up the drawbridge. Build the wall high. Choose your metaphor—it was leadership by fear.

The clock read *7:30*. Time to get going. He scooped up the paper and set the dishes in the sink. He made a last scan of the apartment and noticed the black umbrella by the clock. He wasn't in the mood for small talk, but he felt guilty about the umbrella. He grabbed the card from the table and texted the number.

Sure enough, a few minutes later, the Prius was waiting across the street, sparkling clean in the cold sunshine. The license plate said *SOKRATES*. In the daylight he could see that the car wasn't painted a normal Prius color; it was a shade of gray-green that would be more at home on a BMW or an Alfa. The body was slightly stretched, too, like a limo.

Sokrates sprang from the car and opened the rear door. "Your chariot awaits," he said with a grin. "Punch *Uber Select* on your app to make it official."

David handed him the umbrella with a polite "thank you." He ducked into the back and logged on.

"That's how I get around the draconian rules of high command," said Sokrates. "If you call an Uber without texting me first, you'll get somebody else."

On the night of Andy's summons, David hadn't paid much attention to the interior of the car. Today, nothing about it seemed normal. For one thing, there was extra legroom. And the seats were covered in supple black leather, not almost-leather or looks-like-leather. There was a padded panel between the front seats and back seats that held bottles of water and tubular packs of peanuts in a neat row.

"Help yourself," said Sokrates. "Okay if I call you David?"

"It's Mr. Stone. Tell me, where'd you get the car?"

Eyes up in the mirror. "Did it myself. My last job was a chop shop in Astoria. Worked there fifteen years, since I was a kid. We customized cars for all the honchos. Did the electronics too. If you want privacy for a phone call, just push the button."

David reached forward and touched a horizontal bar positioned flush with the top ridge of the panel. A glass window ascended smoothly, sealing off the passenger compartment from the driver's seat. It was so quiet he could hear music emanating faintly from—where? He touched the button again. The window came down without a sound. "How'd you do all this?"

"Tricks of the trade my friend," said Sokrates. "There's Wi-Fi too. In case you need to Skype or send an email. Normally, a Prius wouldn't qualify for Uber Select, but like I said, I got a dispensation."

David felt a tingle, something akin to awe. Not awe—more like professional respect. Here's a guy who probably hasn't had many advantages in life. Yet he managed to learn this intricate craft. It was ludicrous how much talent was lavished on dead-end jobs. Still, he had to admire the mastery.

"How's that business problem going?" said Sokrates.

David exhaled loudly. "I really can't talk about it."

"You can't talk about your business problem? Then how you going to solve it? Is this one of those things you have to do alone?"

"Yeah, kind of."

Crinkled eyes appeared in the rearview. "Must be *verrry* lonely at the top."

The streets were free of police and protesters that morning. Sokrates pulled the Prius directly up to the entrance of BigSky. David climbed out.

"Thanks for the interesting ride, Mr. Sokouris."

"Call me Sok. The pleasure was mine, Mr. Stone."

David exited the elevator at the top floor and waved amiably as he walked past the receptionist. No reason to alarm the staff. He entered his office, sat down at his laptop, and rescheduled his meetings for the day. He went over to a wide, floor-to-ceiling bookcase and began looking for any advice that might help him rethink the company's strategy.

The problem, as he saw it, was that most business literature had been written for a more predictable time. In a stable business environment, leaders could make leisurely decisions. The lessons of business history were organized into neat rows of case studies, like books on a shelf. Past was prologue. One needed only to look up the correct best practice, and the decision nearly made itself. But the recent election seemed to mark a widespread unraveling of norms.

Constraints he could deal with. He'd learned from his years in architecture that constraints can produce unexpected breakthroughs. Working within narrow boundaries creates a kind of compression that helps you blast through old assumptions. The Sojourner project was a good example. The cost of real estate had been a constraint that kept room rates too high for short-term guests. It forced the design team to question the assumption that a hotel room needed to be at least 150 square feet.

But how could he identify the constraints when the business

climate changed by the hour? He stacked up a pile of books and periodicals that might be of use, and wistfully looked out the window.

Before David came on board, the staffers at BigSky had a magnificent view of the Hudson River. Now their view was the flat surface of a shiny, gold-tinted tower. Looking through the large picture window, all he could see was his warped reflection in miniature, standing alone in his office.

What if he failed to stem the losses? Aside from letting Andy down, he'd be sealing the fate of thousands of employees and leaving the future of BigSky up in the air.

The business press had coined the term *BigSky effect* to describe the way an eco-lodge would trigger an economic boom in any community it entered. It was a win-win for the communities and for BigSky's balance sheet. Meanwhile, the Sojourner business had grown to a third of the company's revenues and nearly half of its profits. Andy's plan had been to use the airport hotels to fund even more of these community-enhancing lodges. But now, instead of the Sojourners funding the eco-lodges, the eco-lodges were draining capital from the Sojourners. The plane was flying upside down, and David seemed powerless to right it.

Something Andy said early on came back to him now: "There will always be storms. You can't change the weather. But you can design your ship and train your crew to withstand the harshest winds you're likely to find."

His mind traveled back to that moment at the restaurant, and how full of hope and excitement they were at the prospect of working together. The contrast with how he felt now churned his stomach. He fought hard against the nausea—there was too much to do.

4

REFLECTION

Saturday, December 4. The previous night he'd had a Daliesque dream of being imprisoned in a huge golden cage, surrounded by scores of shimmering mirrors. Each held a blurred and distorted version of David. He woke up drenched in sweat. He realized it was probably a replicated image from the day before when he caught sight of his reflection in the mirrored Bull Building.

But who was that reflection?

On one hand, it was just David, the kid who grew up on a dairy farm in Washington. His childhood memories were mostly of milking cows and driving the tractor for his father. When he got older, he developed a knack for fixing things—milking equipment, farming tools, the broken-down truck they took to the market—and for building things.

One of his happiest memories was helping his father build a marvelous new barn. It contained a milking parlor, spacious stalls for the cows, streamlined utilities, and a free-feeding system that cut the normal working time in half. On top of walls made from translucent greenhouse siding, they set a soaring, corrugated-steel roof. Instead of supporting the roof with traditional webbed trusses, they used laminated wood beams that hugged the lines of the ceiling, keeping birds from perching in the barn and gobbling up valuable feed. They positioned clerestory windows to catch the prevailing winds, creating fresh, natural ventilation.

In the summers, when work was done, David would sit in the meadow with the majestic peak of Mount Adams rising in the distance. There he'd draw fanciful scenes of farmhouses and city skylines.

But his real passion was baseball. At sixteen he'd rigged up a batter's box in back of the hay barn, with a pitcher's mound the requisite sixty feet, six inches away. The box consisted of a rectangular strike zone painted on an old mattress that hung against the wooden side of the barn. In the corners of the strike zone were smaller rectangles. Off to the sides were silhouettes of batters, one hitting left and one right.

A clever feature of this setup was a cut-down hood from a 1948 Ford, mounted just below the strike zone. When a ball hit the mattress, it dropped into the jury-rigged trough and rolled through a hole to a shallow bucket. When the bucket was full, he'd simply pick it up and walk back to the mound for another round of throws. His parents got used to hearing *thwap*!...*thwap*!...*thwap*!...all summer long as the sound of his pitches punctuated the steady drone of far-off tractors.

At eighteen, just another lanky kid with a mop of wavy hair, David was drafted by the Seattle Mariners and sent to the Tacoma Rainiers, their triple-A club. He quickly became one of the Pacific Coast League's most electric figures. Local sportswriters tagged him "The Slingshot." They said his fastball was so accurate "it could hit corners no one else could see."

Inexplicably, almost before he'd begun, he traded baseball for architecture. He collected his bachelor's degree from the University of Oregon and boarded a plane to New York, taking a job at Shephard & Greene. Then he went on to the untested but highly talented Sestina Partners. It was there, in the Meatpacking District, among the gritty warehouses and cobblestone streets, that his career took root and flourished.

But a résumé is not a life.

Who was he really? David the farmboy-pitcher-architect-CEO? Or David the blurred silhouette in the gold-tinted glass? As a teenager in Washington he was encircled by lively friends and loving parents. During his baseball years he had a steady girl, Stacy. But here in New York, inside the pressure cooker of short deadlines

Reflection

and long days, he knew a serious relationship was out of the question. And now, without the reliable mirror of friends and family, he felt as if he were losing his identity.

The books he'd brought home from the office lay in a pile on the dining room table. He sighed heavily, took one off the top: *Seven Steps to a Winning Strategy*, a book he remembered from his time at Sestina. He flipped to the back for the executive summary:

1. *Gather the relevant facts*
2. *Develop a long-term vision*
3. *Write a mission statement*
4. *Identify the strategic objectives*
5. *Define the necessary tactics*
6. *Determine who is accountable*
7. *Monitor the results*

He set the book on the table, open to the seven steps, and picked up a second book, *Strategy 1-2-3*:

1. *Analyze where you are*
2. *Decide where you want to go*
3. *Determine how to get there*

At least that one had simplicity going for it. He placed it open next to the first book, and picked up a third, *The Strategic Imperative*. This one had five steps festooned with acronyms:

1. *Perform a thorough SWOT analysis*
2. *Locate your BHAG on a 2x2 competitive chart*
3. *Plot SMART goals against a 3-year plan*
4. *Assign KPRs with a spider diagram*
5. *Monitor KPFs on a rolling 12-week basis*

Why can't people speak English? He wasn't sure which was worse: the flagrant use of jargon, or the fact that he actually understood it. Ever since business school he'd been applying these formulas, but with marginal results. He'd already used the seven-step process for BigSky, and this is where it got him. Following a recipe doesn't guarantee a gourmet meal.

A dismal thought occurred to him: he might actually be an imposter—not a real CEO, but a funhouse reflection of one. His failing year at BigSky was Exhibit A.

It was different at Sestina.

For one thing, the company was much smaller—220 people by the time he left. Not an insignificant staff for an architecture firm, but a far cry from the 3,500 people he managed now.

For another thing, Sestina didn't suffer from organizational silos and multiple layers. It was made up of small, fast-moving teams, each dedicated to a temporary project. Players could work on more than one team. When a project was finished, the players would move on to other teams. There was a graceful ebb and flow to the work, and employees had little incentive to stake out political territory.

Finally, there were no board members at Sestina, just partners. Managing the partners wasn't easy—more like herding cats than cows—but at least the cats had a shared vision. He suspected that some of the directors at BigSky would dump the company in a second if they thought they could pocket a quick buck. He tried not to obsess about hidden agendas. But.

He did possess one generalized skill that still might prove useful at BigSky—he was a builder. There was something about building that was a lot like leading a company; if he could tease that out, he might reclaim his confidence. He spent the rest of the day poring through periodicals, textbooks, and blogs, looking for the magic key that could unlock the strategy. And maybe himself.

5

STRATEGY

Sunday, December 5. The world looked better after nine hours' sleep. David got up, slipped into his running shoes, and took off north along the Hudson River. The bare trees and cloudless sky gave the park an antiseptic quality, as if everything had been dry-cleaned and put away for the winter. The only exceptions were scattered runners, and walkers with their dogs and baby strollers.

Some people require the constant companionship of others to feel rooted, to feel alive. David was content to regard people from a distance. He often wondered if that was a drawback in a leader.

He swung around to Ninth Avenue on his way home, slowing to a walk in front of a low building with a wide sidewalk. Above the sign for the Sullivan Street Bakery, he could see the Empire State Building, rising pale blue-gray in the distance. He pushed open the glass door and picked out a fresh loaf of ciabatta. The bread was still warm when he got back to his apartment.

He showered, dressed, and got busy in the kitchen, chopping chives and grating a handful of cheese. For David, Sunday mornings had always meant a big breakfast and the *New York Times*. He pulled a jar of Blue Chair marmalade from the fridge and cut two slices of ciabatta. Donald Fagen's "Nightfly" played on the radio, set to WJAZ-FM. A broad swath of sunshine filled the apartment with buttery light.

Growing up on the farm, his mother had insisted that the boys—meaning he and his father—always have a good breakfast before heading out to the barn. She'd inherited the cooking gene from her Basque-French mother and passed the talent on to David. He loved the physicality of the kitchen—chopping, slicing, mixing, rolling, stirring. And the sensuality too—aromas, tastes, textures. He sometimes wished he could share his love of cooking with someone special, but that experience would have to wait. His focus now was BigSky.

He popped a capsule of Fortissio Lungo into the Nespresso machine and turned around to flip an omelet. His mother taught him the trick: you shove the pan forward as you flip, then pull it back to catch the omelet. He leaned over and inhaled—chives and feta cheese.

The extra sleep had done wonders for his attitude. But there was something else too. The notion that his craft skills—making, fixing, and designing things—might be an advantage in the more abstract world of strategy.

He set the omelet, toast, and coffee on the table, along with a glass of fresh-squeezed orange juice. Fanning out the newspaper, he tossed the main section and opinion pages onto the floor—he wasn't in the mood to read about Richard Bull's latest histrionics.

He glanced briefly at the "Arts" section. The whole scene had begun to bore him—the ridiculous collectors chasing after the latest mutilated animals mounted in oversized vitrines—but now the arts community had come alive in opposition to what it saw as the extreme xenophobia, misogyny, and programmatic cruelty of the Bull administration. Outrage, it seemed, had its advantages.

On page one was a story about a group of artists who banded together to produce a collaborative work on the California coast. It was staged on a wide strip of beach near LAX—a three-hundred-foot-long sand sculpture of the word *WELCOME*. Inbound passengers on flight paths over the Pacific could read the greeting from three miles out. International passengers, upon entering or leaving the terminal, were offered free "welcome pins" in the shape of California, identifying themselves as members of the resistance. Scores of volunteers took donations and collected signatures to fight against what they saw as harsh immigration policies.

Strategy

What David found interesting was not the art or the political impulse behind it. Having lived in the country before moving to the city, he could empathize with both the *pro-* and *anti-* views of immigration. What impressed him was the scale of the collaboration. Artists nearly always work alone. In rare cases, they'll have an assistant or two. But here was a group of artists who had not only managed to work together, but also organize a veritable army of assistants to build, manufacture, and distribute the necessary components.

It was a massive undertaking. First, the artists had to agree on a concept. Then they had to enlist a large number of co-conspirators, perhaps a thousand or more. They had to raise the money, schedule the operation, train the volunteers, and manufacture the various items, all in relative secrecy. A project like this would never be sanctioned by the city.

They'd also have had to build the sculpture under cover of darkness. That meant drawing plans to scale, marking off coordinates in the sand during the day and bringing earth-moving equipment onto the beach at night. Then they had to arrange for a drone to take a photo of the sculpture at sunrise—the same photo he was looking at now—with the hundreds of volunteers milling like ants over huge, letter-shaped anthills.

It made him think: What is strategy, if not a plan for a large group of people to execute a simple idea? It's a type of collaborative design. You start with one reality, imagine a better one, and design a path to it.

Is this something you have to do alone? Sokrates had clearly meant the question to be facetious. Of course corporate strategy isn't something you do alone. It's something you do with a team—the team that will manage the execution.

CEO means chief executive officer, as in *execution*. The strategy can come from anywhere. The role of the CEO is to drive it through on and out into the marketplace.

...ned the last of his coffee, went back to his pile of ...cked out one called *Thoughts on Strategy*. He flipped to a Peter Drucker quote that he'd run across the day before: "The CEO is the link between the inside that is the organization and the outside that is society, markets, and customers." Inside are only costs, he had said. Results were on the outside.

The job of the CEO, then, was to connect the goals of the company with the opportunities in the marketplace—to be the chief *executive* officer, not the chief *everything* officer. David's responsibility wasn't to *create* the strategy, but to set the goals and create the *approach* to the strategy—to build a framework so the team can arrive at a workable solution together.

He shook his head. He'd been trying to do everything by himself. Classic rookie mistake. His go-it-alone attitude had already cost the company five precious days.

BigSky, like most companies, already had a number of teams and taskforces in operation. It also had a permanent executive team. But there was no team specifically formed to redesign the strategy. Their strategy had been a rerun of "The Andy Show," revised and updated for the digital age. David's main concern had been to evolve it, not overwrite it with a new script. But the old script was no longer working.

He reached for a pen and a yellow pad. Okay, who should be on the new strategy team? Tally, certainly. Talia Fortuna had been Andy's chief financial officer from the early days. Unlike other CFOs David had worked with, she understood the difference between a cost and an investment. Moreover, she understood that plus and minus were not the same as right and wrong. Making a profit could be a boon in the short term and a bane in the long term.

Michael Granboy, the chief marketing officer, had to be on the team too. If Tally was all about balance, Michael was about ethics.

Strategy

He would never sacrifice the needs of the public for the needs of the shareholders. It was win-win or nothing. An Oxford-educated Brit, Michael had a habit of quoting Shakespeare at the drop of a hat. They tried not to hold it against him.

David would also want Yasemin Demirci, the company's chief design officer. Yaz was an architect and industrial designer by training, with secondary skills in interior and landscape design. She could not only design hotels, but everything inside and out—furniture, uniforms, gardens, ambient scents and sounds. She was a grand master of the aesthetic chessboard, an integral part of BigSky's competitive advantage. She began as a contractor on the Sojourner project when David was still at Sestina. He hired her on day one of his job at BigSky, creating the CDO role specifically for her.

Then there was Steve Cochran, BigSky's chief operating officer. Steve had been with the company for six years. He had assumed he was next in line for the top job when David was chosen instead. David sensed an air of resentment at first, but Steve seemed to get over it, and did a fine job of managing day-to-day operations. He saw his role as making the trains run on time. BigSky would be lost without Steve's metronomic efficiency.

Should he also include Raven McCanby? As chief revenue officer, Raven was responsible for ensuring predictable inflows of cash. Yet the thought of working with her on strategy gave David pause. Sure, she was a mainstay of the company, but she held strategy and branding in low regard. BigSky's business, for her, was all about putting "heads in beds." In any case, she was traveling at the moment and wouldn't be back for a week.

He sat back, tapping his pencil on his teeth. The five of them should be enough. Better to keep the group lean for now; he could always add more players later.

In the morning he'd call the first meeting of the BigSky

strategy team. He'd have to be blunt about their situation. It was essential that they feel the magnitude and severity of the crisis. Otherwise they might not be willing to make the necessary sacrifices.

Needless to say, they were in for a shock.

6

TEAMWORK

Monday, December 6. David's admin Sandra sent a quick email to the group: Steve Cochran would be tied up in staff meetings all morning. The strategy session would have to wait.

David reminded himself that the business of business goes on, crisis or no crisis. He leaned back in the turquoise Mirra chair he'd salvaged from his days at Sestina. He stared out across the street. As usual, the wide expanse of gold-tinted windows greeted his gaze.

A few years ago, Richard Bull had purchased the building opposite BigSky, a faded Beaux-Arts matron built in 1889 by Charles Follen McKim. Bull told the architects to strip off the limestone ornament and cover the remaining brick surfaces with a curtain wall of glass and steel. They boxed out the windows to bridge the interstitial space between the old and new walls, and masked the floors with spandrel glass—opaque gold to match the tinted windows. This left no trace of the building's actual skeleton, making the floors impossible to count.

Behind the Modernist façade were large public spaces decorated with Versailles-like exuberance. The lobby was littered with overstuffed furniture and overscaled tables supporting huge vases of artificial flowers. The floors were marble checkerboards and the walls gold-flocked patterns of *fleurs-de-lis*. The decor gave the impression of a Hollywood set for *Marie Antoinette*. One critic likened the lobby to "the Grand Bazaar, but without the restraint." Another said Bull's personal apartments looked like "the winnings from a floating casino." Other critics were not so kind.

Bull had raised the new walls of his building thirty feet above the original roofline. This strategy accomplished two goals: inside, it created an atrium with a thirty-foot-high conservatory ceiling; outside, it left a broad expanse of spandrel glass on which he could mount a two-story logo. The atrium housed a huge restaurant space with a dozen glittery chandeliers and a grove of artificial palm trees. The wall outside held four twenty-foot-high gold-painted letters that spelled *BULL*.

In a final strategic flourish, he'd renumbered the floors. He counted the atrium as three floors, the lobby as another three floors, and the lowest level of the basement as floor number one. This made the Bull Building the tallest in Hell's Kitchen, at least numerically. The view from BigSky headquarters was collateral damage.

From the perspective of an architect, the building was a lie from rooftop to basement. There was little integrity in either the design or the motives behind it. But David had learned to be philosophical about such things. You can't stop people from exercising bad taste any more than you can stop them from spewing profanities or spitting on sidewalks. It's annoying when they do it in front of you, but tolerance is essential in a democratic society.

Steve finally confirmed he'd be available after lunch. David used the remaining time to catch up on emails and sign some documents that had collected on his desk.

At 2:00 p.m. the group filed into the small conference room next to his office. They chatted pleasantly, masking an underlying anxiety. Everyone but Yasemin had worked with the others for years. An impromptu meeting like this was rare, and therefore foreboding.

"Thanks for taking time from your busy Monday," David began. "I know you've got a lot on your plates, but there's something urgent we need to talk about." The four executives glanced nervously at each other, eyes darting like startled aquarium fish.

"David, you're scaring us," said Yasemin, using mock panic to disguise real panic. "What is it?"

"I'll get to the point, guys. Last week Andy called me back into the office after work. He told me the board was unhappy with our progress—sorry, *my* progress. He said if I can't come up with a turnaround plan in five weeks, the board would have to take matters into its own hands."

"Into its own hands," repeated Michael. "What does that mean?"

"It means most likely I'll be fired. And by extension, it means a new leadership team and a less optimistic view of the future. Andy wouldn't say so, but he's probably wondering if BigSky's best days are behind it."

Their faces turned ashen.

"That poor man," Talia finally said. "After all those years of building the company, all the ups and downs. He must be agonizing over it."

"I'm a bit worried myself," said Michael.

Yasemin's eyes were black saucers. "Five weeks?"

Steve blurted, "What's going to happen to *us*?"

There it was—the inevitable question. Steve was the one to express it, but they were all thinking it.

David spoke slowly. "Let's not dwell on that for now. We have five weeks, and if we focus too much on the negative, we won't have the stamina to work through the problem. It's obvious that everyone's lives will change if we fail. Let's not fail before we begin." He was sorry as soon as he said it.

"I've had this job for six years," said Steve, voice rising, face in a knot. "During that time I haven't missed a single day of work. And now, all of a sudden, I might be looking for a job?" Yasemin placed her hand on Steve's forearm. He pulled it away and swung his glare toward David. "Why?"

"Steve, we all know the score. Revenues for the eco-lodges are down 22 percent. The airport hotels are holding up, but the travel situation is getting worse. Anything could happen."

"That Bull," growled Michael. "He's wrecking everything. First, he labels the world a dangerous place. Then he tightens security to the point where no one can travel even if they want to. What a wanker." He rose abruptly and strode to the window. The sun had begun to come around to the west and reflected a sickly gold light, the color of yellow tinfoil, into every corner of the room. He pulled the blinds shut.

"You may be right," said David, "but politics isn't our business. We've got a company to run. Let's let Bull do his job, and we'll do ours. Maybe we can start by being honest about our situation. Talia, what's your take?"

She frowned. "I'm sure you saw this morning's flash report. Sales are down. Occupancy rates for the lodges are sagging. Revenue per room is dropping, and so is operating profit. I suppose the trend is even bleaker when you factor in the current political situation. But on the bright side, we've maintained the average daily room rate."

"That's true," said Michael. "Our online reviews are stronger than ever. Customer satisfaction is off the charts."

"What about the Sojourners?" said David.

Talia consulted her laptop. "Occupancy, maxed. Average daily rate, maxed. Customer satisfaction, maxed." She looked up and shook her head. "That's the problem. There's nowhere to go but down. But the good news is, overall, we still have a strong cash position."

David had learned to appreciate the power of free cash flow, a calculation based on operating cash flow minus capital expenditures. He saw it as the single most reliable measure of financial health. Cash gives you room to move. It gives you options. You can expand your business, pay down debt, and take advantage of unexpected opportunities. But he'd also learned—the hard way—that a company facing too many challenges can run out of cash fast.

"Tally, let's be realistic. If Andy and the board are right, we have only 18 months of cash in the bank."

She shrugged. "Maybe, but only if the downward trend continues. In my experience, when things are going well, like two years ago, trouble is right around the corner. And when things are going badly, like now, a turnaround could be imminent."

The whole room seemed to exhale on Talia's insight. What a switch, thought David—a CFO who's more optimistic than the boss.

"Aside from cash," she continued, "we have a healthy real estate portfolio. We've been buying prime tracts of land since the company was founded in 1974. A lot of these properties are in areas that are off-limits to future development—borders of national parks, sensitive habitats, et cetera. Now they're priceless." She made a note. "I'll see if I can find the latest valuation."

"Thanks," said David. "In the meantime, I'd like everyone to go back to your offices and make a list of everything you can think of—I mean everything—that might get the company back on track. Clear your schedules for tomorrow morning and meet me back here. Sandra will send a meeting notice." He got up to leave. As he reached the door, he turned to face his new strategy team.

Teamwork

"Thanks for being here, guys. I couldn't do this alone."

He thought about the phrase he used, "get the company back on track." What did that even mean? All he knew was that their lives would be upended over the next four-to-five weeks. It was anyone's guess whether they'd still have jobs in January. He returned to his office to finish his emails. He glanced at the most recent revenue numbers. As expected, they were dismal. At six o'clock he reached for his phone and texted Sokrates.

Despite the relative calm of Hell's Kitchen after dark, the streets were buzzing with preholiday energy. Sokrates reached up and adjusted the rearview mirror. "Miss me?"

David unbuttoned his overcoat. "Not really. I just figured you needed the money."

"I do this for the companionship, not the money. I get bored running the world from my penthouse on Park Avenue."

"So you're the one," he said with a laugh. "In that case, I have a few questions.

"Shoot."

"What do you think makes a good leader?"

"Ah. I sense trouble in paradise."

"No more than usual," said David, suddenly sorry he'd asked. "I just thought that the great Sokrates, with the benefit of his Uber Advisory Group, could pass along the secret to running the world."

"Asking questions."

"What?"

"Asking questions. That's the secret."

"Could you be more vague?"

"What you're doing right now. Keep asking. Don't settle for easy answers."

A slow smile spread across David's face. The answer to the

question is questions? He wasn't sure if he'd learned anything, but at least he felt better about not learning it.

7

NAYSAYERS

Tuesday, December 7. David stood at the whiteboard with a dry-erase marker. His four teammates sat at the table with their laptops open and their notes ready.

"Thanks for being prepared, everyone. In this first idea session, let's establish one rule, and one rule only—there are no bad ideas. Even suggestions that seem stupid or 'out there' could lead to better suggestions. Let's listen fairly to all of them and try to be creative."

Steve and Talia shifted nervously in their seats.

"Michael, you always have ideas. Want to go first?"

Michael consulted his printout. "Our customer satisfaction ratings are the highest in the industry. I was thinking we could mount a Facebook campaign with targeted offers to previous guests. We've used Facebook before and gotten mixed results, but I think we can do better."

Steve quickly interrupted. "Targeting loyal customers doesn't work for us. We tried that two years ago. Occupancy went up and gross operating profits went down. We need to cut costs first."

"Steve," said David calmly. "Remember? No bad ideas." He wrote *Facebook offers* and *cutting costs* on the whiteboard.

"We could also offer steeper discounts during the off-seasons," said Michael.

Steve rolled his eyes.

David dutifully added *off-season discounts* to the board. "What else?"

"Discounts to travelers visiting more than one hotel, like a carnet." The others looked puzzled. "You know," said Michael, "like when you buy a book of train tickets at a lower price?"

"Carnets," said Talia with a snobby London accent. "Is that a British thing?"

"We're just spitballing," said David. He wrote down *carnets*. "Let's go to Yasemin. Any thoughts, Yaz?"

"We still have cash. What if we build a gorgeous new hotel on one of our undeveloped properties and use it as a focal point for publicity? Maybe we hire a starchitect for the celebrity factor. Frank Gehry, let's say, or Norman Foster."

"Or both. As a team," said Michael.

Starchitects, David wrote. "Keep going."

"Or we could upgrade our in-property retail stores with a line of branded products or clothing."

"Wait," said Steve. "Didn't we decide not to go logo-crazy like that guy over there?" He lifted his chin in the direction of the Bull sign.

"Let's consider it," said David. "Branded products."

Yasemin continued, but with diminished confidence. "This one is a bit long-term. We could remodel our original hotel in Bozeman and throw a gala fortieth anniversary party for the press and industry leaders."

"That could take several years," said David, "but it's a nice idea." He saw Steve's disbelieving stare in his periphery. "How about you, Talia, what do you have?"

"My ideas aren't as fun as Yasemin's. But I looked up our best guess for the value of our real estate assets. We have about 700 million dollars in property value."

A roomful of eyebrows rose in unison.

"We could determine which properties meet two criteria: low

profitability and high appreciation. In other words, if they've gone up in value, but aren't producing strong profits, we sell them off to raise cash. We could use the cash to build more Sojourners."

Yasemin slumped in her chair. Michael leaned forward and put his head on the table, rolling it side to side.

"Only until the tide turns," Talia added quickly. "It wouldn't be permanent."

"All ideas are worth considering," said David, hiding his horror. He wrote down *sell off properties*.

"Or we could reduce our investment in local communities. Going over our records, historically we've invested quite a bit of cash in developing the towns and villages where we draw our workers. I know it sounds awful, but, I don't know, just in the short term…" Her voice trailed off.

My God, thought David. Is this really my team? The greenest intern at Sestina could have come up with better ideas in the first ten minutes.

Steve jumped back in. "I think the real problem isn't the towns and villages, but the workers. We're too generous, especially considering how lazy they are. Sometimes I feel like we're running an entitlement program. They get paid overtime after thirty hours, we give them all kinds of family time, and we never punish them for showing up late. Why don't we do what everyone else does—work them longer, impose more discipline, and penalize them for tardiness. We're not running a charity."

The others gaped at Steve. It was agreed that he was unsurpassed at making the wheels turn; there wasn't a person in the company who didn't respect his ability to grasp all the dependencies among tasks, roles, and assignments. If the company were a rock band, he'd be the drummer. Yet he could rub people the wrong way. He could be arrogant. He tended to throw his weight around with direct reports, as if *he* were the CEO.

Michael could no longer contain himself. "I have to say, that's the worst idea I've heard this morning. Sorry. I know there are no bad ideas, but that one goes against everything we stand for. Turn our workers into serfs? I can't even."

Steve shot back, "And you think your ideas are so great? Social media? Email campaigns? Fucking *carnets*?"

Day one, and the tension had already boiled over. "Okay, everyone—calm down," said David, his voice betraying a growing frustration. "We have to work together if we're going save the company. There's no benefit in getting hot under the collar."

"Look at these ideas," said Steve, waving his hand at the whiteboard. "Discounts, starchitects, branding, anniversary parties. None of these will move the needle. The only tactics that make any sense are to slash our costs or sell off some of our properties."

"That was just an idea," said Talia quietly.

Yasemin jumped in. "I'm not in favor of selling off properties. It's more like selling *out* than selling *off*. Every property we own has the potential to be special, magical. If we just put in a little more effort—"

"Yasemin, dear," said Steve, as if talking to a ten-year-old, "you're hopelessly naïve. You think design is the answer to everything."

"It *is*. More than you know, Mr. Operations." She turned away, face reddening.

"Take it easy on Yaz," said Talia. "We wouldn't have gotten this far without her brilliance." Talia gave Yasemin a conspiratorial nod. "She's our secret weapon."

Look at us, thought David. Our first strategy session and we're already lunging for each other's throats—so much for the no-bad-ideas rule. We can't even handle a simple brainstorming session without breaking into name-calling.

"Listen, I think we're still in shock from absorbing the reality of our situation," he said with deliberate restraint. "This is a lot to take in, and we'll have to learn how to work together. I know for a fact that you appreciate and respect each other. Naturally, we have different views, different opinions, different personal and professional concerns. That's our strength. This is a big challenge, and we'll probably crash into it a few more times before we finally crack it. Why don't we take a break, collect our thoughts, and come back in a day or two?"

They gathered up their notes and laptops and agreed to regroup on Thursday. On the way out, Yasemin shot Steve a poisonous look.

8

TRUST

Wednesday, December 8. David spent the morning on routine tasks. A week of strategy sessions—and, admittedly, wheel spinning—had taken its toll on his to-do list. Sandra had managed to reschedule several of the meetings he'd been forced to postpone. There was one with the general manager of the Sojourner business to review expansion plans, and another with the law firm Culpepper & Culpepper to resolve a dispute over BigSky's Everglades property. There was also a podcast with an interviewer from *Strategy+Business*, asking David to weigh in on leadership qualities—the irony was priceless.

David struggled to give the interviewer something she could work with. He found himself repeating what Sokrates had said the other day. "Keep asking questions. Don't settle for easy answers." She found this viewpoint fresh. She asked him how it played out in his daily decision-making. He lied—he said that decision-making at BigSky was collaborative; that his most important role as

CEO was to stimulate his team's thinking. The truth was the opposite. His whole tenure at the company consisted of business as usual, supplying new ideas with little input from the other executives.

The *S+B* interview threw the situation into high relief. Not only had he not been collaborative, he didn't have a clue about how to foster teamwork. At 7:00 p.m. he texted Sokrates for a ride home.

How odd that people will talk to complete strangers before they'll talk to people they've known for years. They'll open right up to the hairstylist. The bartender. The passenger in the middle seat. David normally resisted chitchat with people outside his immediate circle, but somehow Sokrates was different. More thoughtful. A better listener.

While at NYU, one of the admonitions of his MBA professor was to keep your cards close to the vest. Don't drink with clients. Don't share information with outsiders. With insiders, dispense details on a need-to-know basis. Yet somehow with Sok, David felt the stirrings of trust. He walked through the lobby and found the Prius waiting at the curb. Sokrates held the door for him.

"What's the haps, paps?"

"Hey, Sok. The usual. Back to West Chelsea."

"You got it."

"Listen, I have to thank you for the question you asked last week."

"Which one was that?"

"You asked me if my business problem was something I had to solve alone."

"And?"

"It's not. I was wrong. I've come to the conclusion that it's something I have to solve with my team."

"Makes sense to me, boss—I mean, Mr. Stone." The crinkled eyes in the rearview again.

"Just David."

"Whatever you say."

"I had to admit that I've been managing the company the wrong way. I was in such a hurry to get revenues back on track that I rolled up my sleeves and tried to fix it myself."

"Ready, fire, aim?"

"Something like that. I not only robbed myself of a wider range of ideas, I robbed my leaders of the chance to learn, contribute, and bond. Now I'm paying for it. I've lost a whole year, and I'm down to a month to solve the problem."

Sokrates let out a low whistle.

"Yesterday we finally started to attack the problem as a group."

"How'd that go?"

"Pretty bad. More negativity than creativity. The only thing they could focus on was their jobs. For all I know they've spent the day updating their LinkedIn profiles."

"Wouldn't doubt it. What actually happened?"

David described the brainstorming session, the lack of workable ideas, the disheartening displays of naysaying. It was the opposite of bonding. It was unbonding. They were rats looking for the nearest porthole.

"Tell me," said Sokrates, "do they trust you?"

"Do they trust *me*? The question is: Can I trust *them*? They're so worried about next month and next year that they can't think straight about what's happening now. Frankly, I'm not sure they'll be here in January. I've been spending most of my days in scramble mode, trying to fix the problem myself."

"The reason I ask is, in my experience, trust starts at the top."

"What do you mean?"

"I mean, unless they feel you trust *them*, they have no reason to trust *you*. And isn't that pretty much how you've treated them? Now you've announced this emergency, and they're, shall we say, freaked out."

David slumped back in his seat and ran his hand through his hair. So obvious. Why *would* they trust him? He'd kept them in the dark all year. He'd never asked them to contribute. He'd never asked them to work together creatively. They've found themselves in new territory, under circumstances both frightening and unexpected. He didn't trust them enough to bring them in earlier, and now, in the eleventh hour, he needed *them* to trust *him*.

His phone twitched in his pocket as it gathered up an email. David fished it from his jacket and glanced at the subject line. *Call me*, it said, from av@bigsky.com. No message.

"Excuse me a second." He leaned forward and pressed the button on the padded panel. The window slid up soundlessly as he punched the number. Andy answered.

"David. Just wanted to check in with you. It's been a week since we talked. How's it going? Any progress on the strategy?"

"Hi, Andy. Sorry. I should have kept you in the loop. I'll be honest with you. I've spent most of the week just getting my head around the problem. It's my fault for not taking the time to fully appreciate our predicament. I'm making up for it now. I've pulled together a team from the leadership group and we're banging through some options. Can I let you know in a week or so?"

"I suppose," said Andy, "if that's what it takes. Remember, the clock is ticking."

"I know."

"Is this like the story about Einstein?"

"Which story?"

"Someone asked Einstein what he would do to save the Earth from a meteor that would destroy the planet in an hour. He said he'd spend the first fifty-five minutes thinking about the problem and the last five minutes solving it."

"I'm not Einstein. It may take a little longer."

Cool silence. "Just so you know, the board's getting nervous.

They need to know how you're doing. Our next meeting is in two weeks, the midpoint between now and January 5. I'd like you to come in and make an informal presentation to the group. Can do?"

"Can do." David hung up and pressed the button on the panel. The window slid down.

"Everything okay, boss?" said Sokrates.

"Sorry about that. I guess I have some trust issues after all."

"Perfectly understandable. All my regulars use the cone of silence. That's why it's there, man."

"Listen. Sok. I need to start pulling my team together. Any suggestions?"

Sokrates started to answer, then swerved to avoid a bicyclist with a briefcase strapped to his back. "December nights fall early," he said. "You'd think people on bikes would plan a little better. Buy some reflective gear. Choose a more strategic route."

"Sok, any suggestions?"

He shook his head. "Can't help you, my friend. Spent most of life trying to stay off of teams. It never occurred to me to start one. But let me ask you this: When you think back to the best team you were ever on, one that was really working—I mean, really cooking along—what was it like?"

"Not sure what you mean."

"You know, was everybody an all-star or just an average Joe? Did you practice a lot or just show up and play? Was it like going to work or like coming home from work? Was it fun?"

David gazed out onto the lighted streets and thought back to his baseball days. "We were friends," he finally said.

West Chelsea came into view, followed by the apartment building. When the Prius came to a halt out in front, Sokrates turned to face him. "Don't be so hard on yourself, buddy. Text me. I'll be here for you."

9

KRYPTONITE

Thursday, December 9. Once again, at two o'clock in the afternoon, the team piled into the conference room and began plugging in laptops and shuffling notes. Their faces showed a range of emotions from simple worry to borderline panic. Michael stood up to read from his latest list of ideas.

"Hold on," said David, motioning Michael to sit down again. "Everyone, close your laptops. Relax. I have a different agenda for today's meeting. I'd like everyone to introduce themselves."

They exchanged glances, worry turning to puzzlement.

"It occurred to me that we really don't know very much about each other. Sure, we've worked together, some of us for a long time, but I'd like to go a bit deeper. Get a little more personal." He saw Steve and Michael visibly tense.

"Don't worry, this won't be one of those dopey workshops where you fall backwards into someone's arms or tell the group which car you would be if you could be a car. I just think, if we want to work closely as a team, especially with the stakes as high as they are, we should have a little more context for our relationships."

"I know too much about Steve already," said Talia, flashing a mischievous grin. He returned the favor by jabbing forked fingers toward her, as if to say, "I see you too, toots."

"All right, all right." said David. "I'll go first. Some of you may know this already, but I grew up on a farm near Yakima—"

"Whatima?" shot Steve, drawing a quick laugh.

"Yakima. Washington. Dairy country. I was raised as a cowboy." Good-humored groans filled the room. He described his early interest in fixing things, building things, playing baseball. He made a quick sketch of his pitching invention, explaining how daily practice led to a stint in the minor leagues. He talked about his entry into architecture, his move into management, and the surprise dinner with Andy that landed him in the corner office. "There you have it, folks. The Wikipedia story of me. What about you, Tally? Just a few highlights."

Talia sat upright. Her spiky pixie haircut and hoop earrings had made her the fashion leader of the accounting department. "Well," she took a deep breath, "I didn't play baseball, as you might have guessed. I loved school, and I was fascinated with numbers. I was the teacher's pet. The other girls hated me. My favorite thing was word problems, those math exercises that start out as stories. A farmer has thirty-five sheep and each one eats 8,706 square feet of grass per season. How many acres does the farmer need? That sort of thing."

The others leaned forward.

"My parents died in a car accident when I was sixteen, so I went out and found a job as an assistant bookkeeper. Eventually, I was able to earn a degree in accounting, and then started working for Andy. I've been here twenty-eight years." She suddenly grew quiet, looking at her hands. "And, frankly, I don't want it to end." Eyes welling up, she turned toward Steve.

"Okay, my turn. I did play baseball, but I was crappy at it." This raised a sniffling laugh from Talia. "I switched to boxing in college, and even picked up a few trophies. Winning was everything for me. I doubled down on training—roadwork, free weights, speed bags, sparring sessions—the whole nine yards. Whatever the other guys did, I did twice as hard. It paid off. I ended up at the top of the league. With a broken nose to boot."

"So that's where you get your rugged good looks," said Michael.

"Shut up," said Steve, with a darting feint to Michael's chin.

Yasemin interjected, "Did you know French women have a penchant for rugged-looking men? They call it *jolie laide*, 'beautiful ugly.' So you get movie stars like Jean-Paul Belmondo, Vincent Cassell, Gérard Depardieu, Jean Reno." She tilted her head, gazing at the nooks and crannies of Steve's rocklike features. He definitely fit the mold.

Steve continued, unperturbed. "After college, I went to officer's training school in the Air Force, and ended up in aviation resource management. The only fighting I did was in the ring. After boxing in the Air Force, I went straight into hospitality. Go figure."

David was pleased with this exercise. The team was starting to pull together. They'd stopped obsessing about their problems and were now enjoying each other's company. Keep it going, he thought. "How about you, Yaz? Any boxing in your past?"

"Just retail boxing," she quipped. "I used to design packaging for perfume and cosmetic products in Paris. It was my first job after design school in Istanbul."

"I thought you were Greek."

"Turkish. I spent summers on a little island with my grandparents, where my grandfather was a cabinetmaker. He taught me a lot about design and craftsmanship. After Paris, I moved to New York to study interior design, architecture, and finally engineering. I'm not as good with numbers as Talia is, but I can get by."

"Design, architecture, engineering. Any hobbies to occupy your spare time?" said Michael with a straight face.

"Actually, yes. Magic tricks."

Four heads swiveled in sync.

"You didn't know? Magic! I love it." Her serene face, framed by dark flowing hair, suddenly took on an impish quality.

"Can you give us a demonstration?" said Michael.

"Not while we're working," she said, slightly offended. "And by the way, what's that pencil doing in your hair?"

Michael reached up and pulled a yellow 2B from his brown curls. You could almost hear the jaws drop.

"How did you do that?" said Talia, eyes wide.

"Child's play. I stuck it there while you were admiring Steve's broken nose."

The room dissolved into laughter. David beamed. "Yasemin was on my team at Sestina," he said. "She's the one who figured out how to make the tiny rooms in the Sojourners look much bigger than they really are. It's all about misdirection and fooling the eye. Magician stuff. Brilliant. How about you, Michael? What's your story?"

"Brought up in Brighton," he said, checking his hair for other objects. "Went to university at Oxford. Read politics, philosophy, and economics. Afterwards, I took a junior marketing position with a hotel chain in Islington and worked nights at the ticket office of the Almeida Theatre."

"Is that why you're always spouting Shakespeare?" said Talia.

"Sorry, am I?"

"Sure. Before the meeting. You said, 'The fault is not in our stars but in ourselves that we are underlings.' I Googled it. *Macbeth*."

Michael blushed.

"That's okay," said Talia. "We underlings can mount a coup when the balance sheet looks a little better."

David snorted. "About now I'd be happy to trade jobs with any of you. In the meantime, let's play a little game." He passed around blank sheets of paper. "Write down two things about yourself. First, what your superpower is—the one thing that makes you a good collaborator. Second, write down your kryptonite—the one thing that saps your strength when you're working with other people. Be honest. Everyone has their failings—that's what makes us human. The best teams aren't those that are the most skilled, but those that make the best of being human.

"Next, I want you to do the same for each of the other members, including me. We'll go around the table and describe our own

Kryptonite

superpowers and kryptonites. If someone says one that matches what you've written down about them, shout *bingo*. Ready?"

After a few minutes, they'd finished writing their answers, except for Talia, who finally put down her pen and said, "Done!"

Michael volunteered to go first. He guessed that his superpower was holistic thinking, since he'd always tried to grasp the big picture. He got three bingos. He thought his kryptonite was probably American bad taste, jerking his thumb toward the Bull Building. Bingos all around, and several nods of solidarity.

Yasemin went next. She said her superpower was imagination. She was greeted with a vigorous volley of bingos.

Michael added that it wasn't just imagination, but *practical* imagination, that made her work so magical.

Then she admitted that her kryptonite might be impatience with certain "unaesthetic types." She turned toward Steve and made a face. He raised his arms in mock self-defense. Bingos bounced around like comic-book blows.

"And what about you, Steve?" said David.

"Efficiency," he replied, with perfect efficiency. Four bingos filled the air. His kryptonite? "Change." The group regarded him with newfound respect. A man who knows his weaknesses is a strong man indeed. Admiring bingos were passed around the table.

"What about Tally?" said Michael.

"My superpower is problem-solving," she said, which earned a loud round of bingos. Her kryptonite was a desire for too much safety. The group tried to reassure her that, in the general run of CFOs, she was one of the more adventurous. "Still," she said. Then, turning to David, "And last but not least…"

David looked at his sheet. "I think my superpower—you tell me—is relentless focus." He was rewarded with appreciative applause and four solid bingos.

"You're relentless, alright," said Talia, laughing. "You never get tired of banging your head against the wall." They hooted with recognition—so true. "What about your kryptonite? C'mon, be honest."

"My kryptonite is a lack of patience," he said. With that, the group fell silent. Talia shot a glance at Michael. Michael looked at Steve. Steve turned slowly to Yasemin.

"Yaz, what did you write down?"

Yasemin turned her sheet so Steve could see it.

"Coldness," he read. "Anybody else?"

Talia held up her sheet. "Too remote."

Michael said, "I wrote, 'A bit aloof.'"

Steve held up his: "Coldness."

David threw his head back and gazed upward. Never in a million years would he have imagined himself as cold or remote. He had warm feelings for nearly everyone, didn't he? How could they think otherwise? "Tell me you're joking," he said.

"You have to admit," said Talia, "you're a little on the cool side."

Yasemin chimed in, "You did say to be honest."

"Stone by name, stone by nature," said Michael with a shrug.

David was dumbstruck. He managed to fake a good-natured smile and make a joke about the CEO being the last to know. They agreed to start again fresh in the morning with more ideas. He thanked them for playing the game.

Inside, his heart was in his throat.

10

CIRCLES

Friday, December 10. That morning the rain came down in cold, billowy sheets, coating the streets with a thin layer of ice. Overnight, the temperature had dropped into the teens. David sat hunched in the back of the Prius, bundled in a blue scarf and black wool overcoat. He was blowing on his hands.

Sokrates stopped for a red light at Thirty-Eighth Street. He glanced to the right and saw a ragged young man holding a rough-lettered sign that said: *You are my miracle.*

"Just a sec," he said, jumping out of the car.

David could see Sokrates from the back as he handed the man—more like a teenager—a twenty-dollar bill. The kid threw his arms around Sokrates, burying his head into his shoulder. They said a few words and Sokrates gave him a card. He got back in the car just as the light turned green.

"What did you say to him?" asked David.

"Just a few words of encouragement. You know, I was lucky. I had four or five mentors who opened my eyes to a bigger world. I owe."

David considered this for a moment. "Sok, I need to ask you something. Do I strike you as a cold person?"

"You look like a ball of blue shave ice wrapped in a wool cone."

"That's not what I meant."

"I know what you meant. Listen, you're a little hard to reach. But, hey, you've taken on the whole world. You're in battle mode. And I have every confidence you'll come out a winner."

A small crowd of protesters was converging on the Bull Building. David grabbed his phone and hit the *Times* app. "Breaking News: Bull Blocks Routes to Asia." The feud with China had been brewing for a while. This was more bad news for the travel business. He groaned internally and replaced the phone in his pocket.

"Thanks, Sok," he said. "I can walk from here. See you at six?"

"I serve at the pleasure."

* * *

The meeting started at nine o'clock sharp. David stood at the whiteboard, marker in hand. He called on Michael, who was ready with his list.

"I was thinking a national TV campaign," he said. "A series of thirty-second spots that could do double duty as online promotions—website, YouTube, microsites. Our properties have such stunning locations. We'd be fools not to exploit their visual qualities. So that's one direction.

"Another would be a single, really powerful TV spot for the Super Bowl, like Apple did with its 'Big Brother' commercial. Only now, it really *is* like Orwell's *1984*. We have more surveillance and security and draconian limitations on travel than ever. We need to instill the public with courage. Throw off the shackles! Seek a broader perspective!" He looked around for supporters.

"What would Shakespeare say?" asked Talia, stifling a giggle.

"He'd say, 'Cowards die many times before their deaths. The valiant never taste of death but once!' Wait. You were baiting me."

"Just a little."

Steve said, "Fell for that one."

Michael recovered his poise and continued working down his list. Ideas for a sponsored reality show. Partnerships with outdoor clothing retailers. A frequent-visitor program.

Yasemin offered ideas for a new identity program, localized staff uniforms, and a website overhaul with new social tools.

Talia suggested they shrink the seasons for their extreme weather locations to save on operating costs.

Steve agreed, and dug in on discipline, citing wasteful behaviors that needed to be brought under control.

David was appalled and pleased at the same time. Their ideas were hit and miss, but at least the team was bonding. He wrapped up the meeting and went back to his office, where his smartphone

Circles

shuddered with an incoming text. Sokrates. He suddenly realized it was past 6:00.

The canopy of rainclouds had started to clear, revealing a pale scatter of stars between the buildings. Inside the Prius, Sokrates tapped an imaginary wristwatch. David opened the door and threw himself into the back.

"My apologies," he said.

"I'll send you an invoice. Did I tell you I'm $500 an hour?"

David laughed. He told Sokrates about the team—how they'd finally begun to focus on the task at hand instead of the threat to their jobs. He chalked it up to the exercise from the day before, and then shared a few of the highlights from their personal stories, including his own.

"You really played baseball?" said Sokrates.

"Minor leagues. Ancient history. But the group enjoyed hearing about it. There was one thing I left out, though. Something painful that I've been thinking about lately." He was surprised that he brought this up with a relative stranger.

"Tell Father Sok," said Sokrates with a thick Irish accent. "You'll be protected by the sanctity of the Prius."

David hesitated. Slowly, with some trepidation, he told Sokrates the story of his last Triple-A game. He'd been pitching against the Rainiers' biggest rival in the final matchup of the season. His team was up by one run in the eighth, but the home-plate umpire had in for him. All day long he'd been calling anything on the corners a ball. David had already walked a batter, who then scored on an outfield error.

He was facing Darrel Kapka, not only one of the league's best hitters, but the surliest player David had ever seen. Kapka thought nothing of screaming at a spectator or spiking the shins of an unsuspecting shortstop. The count was 1-0. A walk would place the go-ahead run on base with only one out. Kapka backed out of the box and pointed his bat toward the mound. "C'mon, milk boy." His face contorted into a sneer. "You're losing it. You couldn't hit the side of a barn."

David could feel his temper rising. He looked in, shook off the catcher's sign. The umpire growled, "Speed it up, Stone. Play ball." David went into his windup and threw a perfect slider to the heart of the strike zone. The catcher never moved his glove.

"Ball!" cried the ump.

David caught the return throw with a snap of his glove. He shook his head in disgust. The count was 2-0. He could still recover. He looked in to the catcher for the sign. Curve. He placed his second finger along the seam of the ball.

"I had your girlfriend last night," taunted Kapka, shouting over the boos of the crowd. "She's not as good as your team said she was." Raucous laughter issued from Kapka's dugout.

David's jaw clenched. *That's baseball. Don't lose your cool.* He flashed a glance at Stacy sitting with her parents in the stands. She showed no reaction to Kapka's slur. He leaned back and then unwound. His hand came down sharply, releasing the ball at the optimal point. The pitch broke at the last second for a backdoor strike.

"Ball!"

The bad call was like a match to dry tinder. The heat started in his legs and laddered up his frame. He violently turned and kicked the mound. *Calm down. The umpire is not the enemy.* He slowly leaned in to get the sign from the catcher. By now he felt as if he were no longer the occupant of his own body.

Kapka smelled blood. "Hey, milk boy. Who's humping your dago-frog mom while your dad's out milking the cows?"

David went from red-hot anger to ice-cold calculation. He threw without a windup. A 95-mile-an-hour fastball sailed directly to the center of Kapka's helmet, knocking it off toward the backstop. The big man crumpled to the ground like an empty uniform. He lay there motionless. Players and coaches rushed the plate. An emergency team carried Kapka off the field on a gurney. There wasn't a fan in the Northwest who thought the pitch was an accident, not with David's command of the ball.

He knew right then he was finished.

It didn't matter that Kapka had escaped death with a severe concussion and a cracked skull. It didn't matter that the scandal would eventually fade, just another yellowed clipping in a scrapbook. What mattered was that David knew he was dangerous on the field. A time bomb. He could control his pitches, but he couldn't control his temper. He quit baseball on the spot, consciously pushing his emotions so far down that they could never rise to the surface again.

Sokrates nodded. "You think that's why people say you're cold?"

"Probably. But it's better than unleashing the kind of rage that kills people."

"Anger has to go somewhere, man. Better to channel it than bury it. That stuff can poison you." Sokrates skirted a stalled delivery van and returned to the right lane. "Can I tell you a different baseball story, also protected by the sanctity of the Prius?

"Sure," said David.

"I grew up in Queens. The bad part. By the time I was twelve, most of my friends were already in gangs. My mother said she'd gouge my eyes out if I joined one. She watched me like a hawk. My father was long gone—who knows where—and she was raising me on her own. My friends and I were forever dodging Crips, Bloods, and Latin Kings on one side of the law, and brutal cops on the other. It made sense to join up, if only for protection. But I didn't."

"Why?"

"My mother trusted me," said Sokrates with a shrug. "One

night at the park I saw a Blood kill a kid from our neighborhood gang. On the baseball diamond. And I knew he saw me. I ran back and pulled a gun—a loaded Glock nine-millimeter—from under the stoop in front of the kid's house. I took it home and taped it to the bottom of my bed."

David sat up, horrified.

"Three days later, just after midnight, I woke up to a crash in the living room. The killer had broken through the door and was screaming at my mother: 'Where is he? Where's that fucking snitch?' She yelled back at him, but he started swinging and wouldn't stop."

"What did you do?"

"I shot him. Untaped the Glock and shot him."

David's mouth fell open. He thought *his* secret was dark. This one was pitch black. He'd never complain about his calm, quiet life again.

"What happened?"

"Oh, you know, the usual—cops and hearings and reporters all over the place. The guy didn't die. They carted him off to Rikers where he could hang out with his Blood brothers on a permanent basis. I was underage, and the whole thing blew over. A few years later I got a job at the custom car shop and we moved to a better part of town. No one bothered us again."

"So you escaped the downward spiral."

"That's the biggest problem with neighborhoods like mine. No one wants you to leave. Your friends treat you like you're some kind of traitor. It's like, 'What—we're not good enough for you?' They won't let you graduate, if you know what I mean. They're terrified that you might get something, or go someplace, that they don't have access to. The whole neighborhood keeps spinning in the same circles. It's hard to get out."

David nodded.

"Speaking of circles," said Sokrates. "How's your new team doing with the strategy?"

"Ah. Well. They're bonding better, but their ideas are all over the place." He let out a low sigh. "I think we're too close to the problem. In fact, we're *inside* the problem. If we don't solve it pretty soon, we'll drown in it. Makes it difficult to concentrate."

"Have you thought of expanding the circle? Opening it up? Maybe adding a ring to the outside?"

"What do mean?"

"Up to you. Teamwork makes the dream work."

When David finally got out of the car, the air was cold and clear. The light from the city couldn't dim the winter stars that sparkled like tiny diamonds. He waved to Sokrates as the car disappeared into the night.

11

MAYDAY

Saturday, December 11. Sokrates had unlocked the door to a room of painful memories, then neutralized them by sharing even more painful memories of his own. David could only imagine the trauma, fear, and self-recrimination that a twelve-year-old Dmitri Sokouris must have suffered in the aftermath of such violence. If Sokrates could survive the memory of those dark days, David could certainly get past a minor league sports scandal.

Sok was right—David and the team had been swimming in too tight a circle. They were like fish that had no idea they lived in a fishbowl. Hell, they couldn't even grasp the concept of water. They desperately needed to escape the aquarium if they were ever to find a way forward. Here they were, halfway to the first presentation to the board, and all they had was a handful of random ideas.

His mind drifted back to baseball. He thought of Gard Scott, his catcher in the early days. Gard was older than David and steady with a glove. Whatever David threw at him, Gard could catch it.

About a year before the Kapka scandal, Gard quit the team to get his MBA at the Haas School in Berkeley. He started a consulting firm in Silicon Valley called Cultura, racking up an impressive number of successes with tech companies and other organizations.

David grabbed his laptop and Googled *Cultura*. Up popped the company's home page. The headline, "Designing the Way Forward," ran across a changing series of images—executives writing on whiteboards, a creative team building prototypes, customers interacting with products, a CEO addressing an audience of analysts. Along the top were links for *Strategy*, *Brand*, *Culture*, and *Thinking*.

Under *Thinking* were several articles written by Gard and by a partner named Shigeru Morita, along with one-offs by other members of the firm. A particular piece caught David's attention: "Design Thinking as a Strategic Tool." Shigeru Morita made the case for a planning approach that swaps the traditional analytical process for one closer to the way creative people work. This was something David could relate to. He'd always wondered why strategy couldn't be designed, not just decided.

He clicked the "About Us" link and found several recommendations from highly regarded CEOs. He wondered how much it would cost to engage a group like Cultura. Whatever it was, he could weigh it against the very real possibility of losing the company.

Fighter pilots use the word *mayday* whenever they have an emergency. It comes from the French *m'aider*, which literally means "help me." He decided to make that distress call now. He looked up Gard's phone number on the website. He fully expected to reach a recording on Saturday morning, but after a few rings, Gard himself picked up.

"David!" he cried. "A blast from the past! How's the old Slingshot? Playing any ball?"

David filled him in on the last fifteen years—his winding path through architecture, business school, and now the CEO-ship of BigSky. He admitted that none of this would have happened if it weren't for his run-in with Darrel Kapka.

"I read about the beanball," said Gard. "Had it coming, if you ask me. Ugly face, ugly attitude, ugly everything. What an asshole. Shit—I promised Heather I'd tone down my language. Anyway, today he's a washed-up minor leaguer and you're running the coolest company on the planet. Revenge is sweet."

David wasn't so sure. He brought Gard up to speed on BigSky's predicament and the team's inability to crack the strategy problem, all against the background of a darkening business climate.

"Five weeks?" he said. "Really? How many weeks left?"

"A little over three."

"And what's the deliverable?"

"A strategic plan. If they think it has promise, they'll fund whatever we need to take it to the next stage. If not, well…"

"You're fucked, I get it." said Gard. "How's your group holding up?"

"They're freaked out, but they haven't bailed yet. I'm just not sure I can get their best work under these circumstances."

"Need a hand?"

"I thought you'd never ask."

"Tell you what. I can have a small team in your office Monday morning at nine o'clock. I'll lead it myself. We have a strategy framework that cuts the planning process to about 20 percent of the usual time. It's a bit—shall we say—intense, at least for some execs, but you'll be fine. Your experience as a designer will give you an advantage."

"Gard, you're a lifesaver. How much are we talking about?"

"I'll get you a rough estimate on Monday. We can base it on three of our senior people for three weeks, plus an extra two or three of us for the home stretch. We'll need to shuffle our schedules a bit, so there'll be a small upcharge for that."

"Understood."

"Who's on your team now?"

David went down the roster, detailing the strengths and weaknesses of each member, and giving examples of the ideas they'd come up with.

"You don't have a head of sales, somebody like that?"

"Raven McCanby. She's our chief revenue officer. She and Steve just about ran the company before Andy stepped back. I haven't put her on the team because she's traveling, and because she doesn't have much patience for marketing and design. And branding—well, she thinks branding is the spawn of the devil. She and Michael are oil and water. Yasemin gets a rash whenever Raven walks into the room."

"She has to be there," said Gard flatly. "She's ground zero for the declining revenues. You can't just cut her out. Let's get her on the team as soon as she's available. I'll try to keep the players from strangling each other."

David was dubious. Raven had gotten defensive every time the subject of sales came up. She took it personally. Still, he was happy to have Gard's help, and agreed to the request. "Anybody else?"

"You should probably invite your chief information officer and your general managers for the two main businesses. Also their VPs for both guest services and concierge services."

"We don't have concierge services for the Sojourners, but I can round up the other VPs and GMs."

"Okay, twist their arms. That gives us twelve from BigSky and three from Cultura. We'll break into three teams of five for the exercises."

David expressed his gratitude to Gard for jumping in on such short notice. In fact, he was half-drunk on a cocktail of joy, relief, and wild anticipation that they might actually make some progress after ten days of flailing.

He'd email Raven and the others first thing Monday to check on their schedules. Better yet, he'd do it right now.

12

CHOICES

Sunday, December 12. The Weather Channel had promised rain and was as good as its word. The muted clatter of water on windows masked the sound of light Sunday traffic, the white noise providing a soothing background for reflection. David rested his feet on the newspaper-heaped coffee table, a café au lait waiting on his Aalto side table. He'd slept well the night before. Gard's gracious offer was a balm to his battered psyche.

On the sofa beside him lay an old scrapbook his mother had secretly kept for him. She surprised him with it the day he'd left for architecture school. Truthfully, it was the last thing he wanted to bring into his big new life and his tiny new apartment. But Mom. Such a sweetheart. He had dutifully moved the scrapbook from apartment to apartment, though he had never unpacked it. It bulged with the ephemera of a boy's life, lovingly displayed in old photographs, report cards, awards, blue ribbons, and aging newspaper articles.

He picked it up and placed it on his lap. On the cover, the words *Our David* were written in careful calligraphy. He opened to the first page. In the middle was a small black-and-white photo of a six-month-old baby with a goofy grin. A small caption proudly proclaimed, *First Tooth*. The pages overflowed with a mother's love and pride.

Undoubtedly, Sok's mother was equally loving and equally proud, but how different the lives of the two women must have been. David's mother had enjoyed the relative stability of a steady marriage and work-filled days on the farm. Her son was safe as long as he was careful around the livestock and machinery.

Sok's mom, on the other hand, led a more precarious existence. She raised Dmitri alone on a single mother's wages, just enough to afford a shabby apartment in a rough part of Astoria. She probably worried every time he was out of sight, knowing the streets weren't safe for adults, much less children. The men in her life were apparently less-than-reliable. Sok's dad had disappeared before he could make a first impression. For Sokrates, there was no father figure, no idyllic farm, no fondly curated scrapbook.

David turned the pages, past the crayon drawings of cows and tractors, past his first attempts at architectural sketching, past the plan he drew for the milking barn. He finally came to the baseball section he knew would be there. This was the reason he'd never pulled the book from the box all these years. But now he felt ready. Compared with Sok's roller-coaster life, his own was a gentle push on a park swing.

Here were photos of David in his Little League uniform. Playing second base in Pony League. Pitching for an American Legion team. He turned the page and saw a nineteen-year-old boy, all teeth and bones, after his first winning season as a pitcher. His girlfriend Stacy had stretched up and planted a kiss on his cheek for the camera.

David closed his eyes.

He carefully turned another page and came to the dreaded

clipping. The headline had been removed, but he could still see it in his mind's eye: "Tacoma's Slingshot Nearly Slays Batter." The photo, sliced from a news clip, showed Darrel Kapka flipping backward, helmet flying through the air. The story couldn't have been more lurid. It told of David Stone, farm-boy-turned-phenom-turned-would-be-killer:

> The hotheaded hurler from Tacoma unleashed his considerable temper in the form of a fastball to the forehead of batter Darrel Kapka. Kapka couldn't get out of the way of the 95-mile-an-hour bullet and sustained a sickening crack to the skull. He remains in critical condition at St. John's Hospital in Seattle.

Another mother might have buried this episode. Not David's. She put the clipping there specifically for him. He could still remember her terse advice: "When you make a mistake, David, learn from it."

He closed the scrapbook and gazed at the rain coursing down the windowpane. Kapka was a jerk, certainly, but he didn't deserve to die. David suddenly wanted to find him and apologize, make some sort of amends. No matter how much they'd hated each other on the field, in some bizarre way they were brothers.

Some say people's lives are defined by the choices they make. But sometimes choice doesn't come into it. Sometimes all people get is a split-second to react, and their programming takes over. David didn't decide to hit Darrel Kapka. He just did it. But what about the decisions he *had* made, like bailing at the first sign of trouble? What if he'd stayed in baseball? What would his life look like now? A little less lonely? More successful? Would he bail on BigSky too?

He thought about Andy's words, not so different from his own mother's. *It's on you. Your moment of truth.*

Bringing in Gard, while a relief, also made him uncomfortable. It felt like ceding control, an abdication of leadership, an admission of failure. He only knew Gard as a catcher, not as a consultant. As a catcher, he commanded the infield. He was the team's chief defensive strategist, directing the game from his position behind the plate. Would he try to direct the strategy for BigSky? Would he lead the group someplace David wouldn't want to go?

Tomorrow would tell.

13

FIVE Qs

Monday, December 13. The conference room was crowded, the mood electric. The two GMs had managed to clear their schedules and so had their VPs. The only person who couldn't attend was Raven. She was still in Fiji evaluating a property for a future eco-lodge.

David stood up and introduced Gard to the BigSky team. Gard, in turn, introduced his two colleagues, strategist Shigeru Morita and researcher Cary Blank. These three would bring structure to the strategy effort, leading the group through a series of intensive exercises. Gard warned of long days and periodic frustration.

"I won't lie to you," he said to the group. "This is real work. But we'll try to have some fun too. The fact is the deadline for the presentation is tight—only three weeks from now. Some of you will have to hang in there through the holidays. We'll know more about the schedule after we get into the work."

He went over to the whiteboard and grabbed a marker. At the

top of the board he wrote *Five Qs*. He turned back to the group. "Strategy isn't easy," he said, "but it *is* simple. All we have to do is answer five little questions." He wrote them on the whiteboard:

1. WHAT IS OUR PURPOSE?
2. WHO DO WE SERVE?
3. WHERE SHOULD WE COMPETE?
4. HOW WILL WE WIN?
5. HOW WILL WE GROW?

He tapped the board with his marker. "Simple, as I said. But far from obvious. For example, can anyone define the word *purpose*?"

The participants exchanged glances. Sojourner's GM ventured an answer: "Like a vision or mission?"

"Not exactly. People talk about vision, mission, and purpose as if they're interchangeable, but they're not. We need to be precise." He turned to the board and drew a pyramid divided into three levels:

"At the top of the pyramid is purpose. Your purpose is why you're in business beyond making money. *Beyond making money.* It drives everything else, and it never changes."

"Wait," interrupted Steve. "Shouldn't making money be at the top of the pyramid? Isn't that the purpose of a business? What kind of company is beyond making money?"

"Think about it," said Gard. "If a company is focused on financial profit to the exclusion of everything else, what happens when they haven't made a profit in a while?" He looked around. "Anyone?"

Yasemin raised her hand. "They give up."

"Right. They say 'screw it.' They quit. They look for another way to make a dollar and the cycle begins again. But if they're committed to a larger purpose, they're much more likely to stick it out. They'll keep trying different approaches until they achieve that purpose."

"I'm not sure I agree with that," said Steve.

"Objection noted," said Gard. "Now, at the middle level, below purpose, are two related concepts: *mission* and *vision*. Both of these answer to purpose. They can last anywhere from five to twenty years. A mission is an ambitious goal for achieving a purpose.

"Closely related to mission is vision. You can think of vision as the *visualization* of your mission. Microsoft, for example, had declared that its mission was 'to lead the personal computer revolution.' But its vision was 'a computer on every desktop and in every home.' Can you visualize the computer on the desktop? The second level of the pyramid gives you two views of the same goal. They're like fraternal twins. Are you with me so far?"

"What are Microsoft's mission and vision now?" said Talia.

Gard scratched his head. "Shit, I should know that. Pardon my French. I suppose they're struggling like you are. They've been lapped by their old rival, Apple, whose strategy has always been clearer and more focused."

"What's Apple's purpose?" asked Michael.

"They've said their core purpose is to 'build tools for the mind that advance humankind.' A purpose never changes, so if they ever stopped building tools for the mind, or stopped trying to advance civilization, Apple would be a different company."

"I'm not buying it," said Steve. "A public company's purpose is to increase shareholder value. Period. Anything else is irresponsible—and probably illegal."

Five Qs

"Steve," interrupted David quietly. "Let's keep an open mind and see where this goes."

Steve scowled and slouched in his seat.

Gard continued. "Underneath the twin concepts of mission and vision are the goals you need to accomplish them. These would be completed in, say, one to three years. Finally, underneath the goals are all the daily and weekly tasks to accomplish the goals. Got it?"

They nodded. Talia raised her hand. "Our company isn't Apple or Microsoft. Those are huge technology companies, and we're just a medium-sized hospitality company. Do the five *Q*s really apply?"

"Absolutely," said Gard. "They're universal. They apply to consumer companies, business-to-business, service companies, product companies, public companies, private companies, small companies, large companies, nonprofits—all types of organizations. They even apply to individual careers. They're what you might call the foundational principles of strategy."

Talia nodded, adjusting her glasses.

"Now, let's break into teams and try to define BigSky's purpose. I'll turn the meeting over to Shig, who can lead us through the first exercise."

Shigeru Morita was a trim Japanese-American in his early forties. He stood up and scanned the room, counting. "Okay, it looks like we have fourteen people, so let's break into two teams of five and one team of four. We'll put one Cultura person on each team."

He asked David to choose the teams with an eye to variety, and handed out exercise sheets. The first exercise called for everyone to imagine that twenty-five years from now the company has gone out of business. Their task was to write a glowing obituary, extolling its contributions to the world.

"Two of the teams can find other spaces to work more privately, and one can stay here. You've got forty-five minutes. At the end of that time, I want someone from each team to read their obituary to the rest of the group."

"Does it have to be realistic?" asked Michael.

"It has to be big, bold, and courageous," said Shigeru. "Let's suspend our judgment about what's realistic. Okay, go."

The teams returned ninety minutes later, after begging Shigeru for extra time. They'd written their obituaries on large sheets of paper and were now sticking them to the whiteboard.

The first two obits were fairly predictable. They assumed that the success of the company would continue in a straight line once it got back on track. The third, however, was a complete fantasy. Shigeru asked for a spokesperson from that team to speak for the group. Michael stood up and read their statement:

> *The world went into mourning last Friday when it learned that BigSky, Inc., the most successful lifestyle brand of all time, had finally closed its doors. The company, founded in 1974 by visionary Andrew Vineyard, had opened the possibility of eco-travel for every man, woman, and child on the planet. Not only did it design and build spectacular hotels in far-flung locations, it made travel easier for everyone. People who could not afford airfare or the cost of a*

Five Qs

> *hotel could nonetheless experience the magic of travel through virtual reality and other advanced media—to be determined.*

He was interrupted by good-natured jeers. He soldiered on, his British accent adding gravitas.

> *After 75 successful years in business, BigSky had built 700 eco-lodges; 245 airport hotels; a travel-based TV network; an international school system for its local communities; and a major university focused on ecological studies, comparative sociology, and sustainable design. The company was credited with saving the coral reefs, ending third-world hunger, and eliminating malaria, dengue fever, and dysentery. When asked by this news outlet how they managed the vision and courage to push to greater and greater heights, 60-year-old CEO David Stone…*

Laughter punctuated his reading as they pictured David with gray hair.

> *…said he had looked to Shakespeare for guidance: 'Our doubts are traitors,' he quoted, 'and make us lose the good we oft might win by fearing to attempt.' Today we salute the passing of a grand corporate citizen, one who never feared to attempt, and in attempting, vanquished all trace of doubt. Having achieved its purpose, the company will convert their properties into wildlife centers where citizen scientists can study local ecosystems. Our children and our children's children will rise up and say the world is a better place because of BigSky.*

The room exploded with cheers. Michael mimed an Elizabethan

bow, complete with multiple flourishes.

Shigeru stood and walked to the head of the room. "Well done, Team Three! Okay, pretty crazy stuff. Now I have a question for you." He paused to take in the room, his glance resting briefly on each participant. He slapped his palm against the obituary on the whiteboard and said, "Why don't we do this?"

The laughter died as the group realized he was serious. Talia finally spoke up. "Because, like you said, it's crazy stuff."

"Is it?" said Shigeru. "Or does it just *seem* crazy because it's so far from where we are now? Remember, we have twenty-five years to accomplish something of this magnitude. What's stopping us? Is there anything physically or logically impossible about these goals?"

Heads shook "no." David smiled. If strategy were a racecar, the driver had just stomped on the gas pedal. He felt a rush as the meeting accelerated.

"Okay, then, let's keep thinking big," said Shigeru. He passed out another exercise sheet. "Go back to your teams and write a purpose statement. Twenty-five words or less to remind ourselves of why we're in business beyond making money."

When they came back, each team had written a statement capturing the bold aspirations of the obituary. They discussed which parts of each statement were the most inspiring. Cary, from Cultura, went to the board to write out a composite statement. She was a thirtyish blonde with her hair cut in a blunt bob. A red barrette held a clump of wayward bangs in place. She copied the statement onto a large sheet of paper and stuck it up on the whiteboard. "Okay," she said, "here's what we've got so far":

> *Our purpose:*
> *To democratize travel so that more people can extend their boundaries, embrace new cultures, and enrich their understanding of the world.*

"Extend, embrace, enrich," she read. "Does that sound right?" There were murmurs of approval here and there, and isolated applause.

David said, "What if we shortened it? How about 'to democratize life-enhancing travel'? All we're saying is two things: first, travel makes your life bigger and better; and second, BigSky wants to make travel possible for everyone."

"That's not bad," said Michael. "And one reason it's life-enhancing is because, in traveling broadly, you learn more about your own country. There's a saying in Great Britain: 'What can he know of England who only England knows?'"

"Shakespeare?" said Talia.

"Kipling."

"Show-off."

They spent another half hour debating and refining the purpose statement. Gard finally brought the session to a close. "Why don't we sleep on it tonight. I know you've got a shitload of work waiting for you. Damn. I've got to stop swearing," he said, to laughter from the group. "Tomorrow we can address the second *Q*, about who we serve. Kick-ass work, everyone."

David was pleased, not to mention relieved. They'd made more solid progress in one day than they had in the whole previous week. He'd never think of BigSky in quite the same way again. He stood up to shake Gard's hand.

"Let's have a round of applause for Cultura," he said. The group complied. "And thanks to all of you for your amazing ideas. I know we're on our way to an exciting strategy."

It looked like Gard would be just the savior David needed. He marveled at how much people can grow, given enough focus and effort. He'd known Gard as a minor-league catcher, but now he was an accomplished strategy leader with an international reputation. Shigeru handed David an envelope. The estimate showed that Cultura's help wouldn't come cheap. But it compared favorably with larger consulting firms, especially in light of David's last-minute request.

As they left the meeting, he mentioned to Cary how impressed he was with Cultura and its accomplished founder. "How is he to work for?" asked David.

"In Gard we trust," she said, flipping back a strand of blonde hair.

14

TRIBE

Tuesday, December 14. The next morning the group returned to find a poster-size printout of the company's purpose statement taped to the wall of the conference room. Next to it was David's abbreviated version:

> *Our purpose:*
> *To democratize life-enhancing travel.*

On a table in the corner were bagels with various toppings, a selection of pastries from La Patisserie Renaud, and a large urn of Blue Bottle coffee. David asked the team to bring their breakfast plates to their seats so the session could begin.

Gard stood up as the group settled in. "Today we'll work through the second strategy question, about the customers we're serving. The topic of customers brings us straight into the realm of branding. Can anyone tell me what a brand is?" He looked around.

"Logos and stuff," said Steve.

"Anyone else?"

"Marketing and advertising?" offered Talia.

Michael spoke up. "I define it as the sum total of all the messages a company sends to customers."

"A promise of quality?" ventured Yasemin.

Gard went around the room and got similar answers from the GMs and VPs. Everyone looked expectantly to Gard for the correct answer.

"All those definitions are what I would call TBFU—True But F-ing Useless. A better way to define the word *brand* is to look at it from the customer's view. A brand is a customer's understanding of a product, service, or company. In other words, it's about *them*. It's what *they* say it is, not what *we* say it is."

A dozen eyes stared blankly. Another dozen examined the ceiling, as if evaluating the placement of the air ducts.

Steve exhaled noisily. "Why are we talking about branding anyway? I thought we were looking for a business strategy."

"Because brand and business are inseparable," said Gard. "Consumers have real-time information about their choices—competitors, pricing, features, everything. They hold the cards. The only way *we* can win is for our *customers* to win. Business strategy is about what the company needs from customers to succeed. But brand strategy is about what our *customers need from us* to succeed. They're two sides of the same coin."

He was greeted with blank looks.

"Okay, think of strategy as a plan to create customers."

"Create customers?" said Talia. "How do you do *that?*"

"By co-designing a product or service that improves their lives. When they experience the benefits, they tell their friends. That creates the brand. The brand, in turn, drives our continued success. It's so fucking simple. Shit, I promised my wife I wouldn't swear."

Talia winced.

"What I mean is," he said, "it's extremely comprehensible. Here, I'll show you." He grabbed a marker.

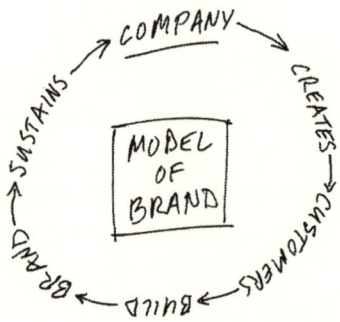

"At the top, we create the customers. We do this by working closely with customers to design our products and services. In turn, they create the brand—remember, it's what *they* say it is, not what *we* say it is. The brand, once created, sustains the company. It's a virtuous circle. Companies are usually so focused on internal goals—costs, profits, processes, employees—that they forget that customers are the whole reason they exist."

"I think I get it," said one of the ceiling inspectors. "Your brand is like your reputation."

"Yes! A commercial reputation. And like any reputation, you can't totally control it. All you can do is behave in ways that encourage people to understand you, like you, and trust you."

Yasemin raised her hand. "Well, I'm not sure *I* get it. Why is that definition better than the others?"

"Because now we have a basis for measuring success. It's easy to gauge the effectiveness of a logo or an ad campaign or a website interface, but none of this will tell us if we're winning where it counts—in the hearts and minds of customers. The only useful measurement of a brand is what customers say behind our backs."

"Who cares?" Steve shrugged. "You can't please everyone."

"True. But we need to make sure we please enough of the right people to keep growing the business. Take an example," said Gard, walking over to the window and opening the blinds. "People talk a lot about the Bull brand. Using our definition, what kind of brand is it?"

Hands shot up all over the room.

"Hotels and golf courses for the wealthy," said a Sojourner VP.

Michael said, "Trophy properties for tasteless oligarchs."

"A financial house of cards," said Talia with a knowing smirk.

"The sweet smell of success," said Steve, closing his eyes and filling his lungs with air.

Other participants suggested "a family dynasty," "the gold standard of condo development," and "the essence of Ugly American."

"As you can see," said Gard, "there are as many opinions in this room as there are people. And that's okay. You don't need to please everyone to have a brand, as Steve pointed out. All you need is enough believers to build the brand and grow it.

"But you also need to pay attention to the kind of people you attract. Your customers are your tribe—the army of people who volunteer to support you, buy from you, and tell their friends about you. If your tribe is weak, or stingy, or disloyal, it doesn't bode well for the long-term viability of your brand."

"What if your tribe is a load of good-for-nothing opportunists?" said Michael, jerking his head toward the Bull Building. This set off a spasm of laughter.

"In that case, I would say the long-term outlook is bleak. Which doesn't mean that the short-term results couldn't be spectacular. But BigSky is in it for the long haul. So let's decide exactly what kind of customers we need to get us where we're going. Doctor Blank can lead us through the exercise."

"Doctor Blank," said David, eyebrows raised. "You're a PhD?"

"My first name is Doctor," said Cary, deadpanning. The members looked at each other. "Just kidding. I have a doctorate in research science." She smiled, and handed worksheets to the participants.

"My job is to keep us all grounded in actual customer needs."

The assignment called for listing as many traits as possible to describe the ideal customers of BigSky hotels. These included not only demographics like age, gender, race, education, professional status, geographic region, and income level, but also psychographic insights about values, attitudes, interests, personalities, and lifestyle.

"Okay, everyone. You know the drill. Forty-five minutes with your team, then you'll read back your answers to the whole group."

A VP for the eco-lodges raised his hand. "Are we talking about the customers we have now, or the customers we'd like to have in the future?"

"Let's go with current customers, so we have a baseline for change." She looked around. "Any more questions? No? Let's go."

An hour later the participants filed back into the conference room, sheets brimming with notes.

"Who wants to start?" said Cary.

Steve's team urged him to present first. He stood to face the group. "Our customers are twenty to seventy years old, so it's a pretty wide range. They're equally male and female, yet the decision-makers tend to be female. They're mostly white and college-educated, with white-collar jobs and homes in cities or suburbs.

"Their psychographic profiles suggest they're curious, adventurous, social, and like to keep fit. They're more interested in doing things than having things, meaning they'd rather take a vacation than buy a new wardrobe or an expensive piece of furniture." He looked smug as he sat down. "What did you guys come up with?"

The two other teams went in turn. All three had similar views of their current customers.

Cary stood and walked to the front of the room. "It's great that you all agree. But if these are truly your customers, we have a problem."

The participants looked puzzled. Shig made a gesture with his hands that said, "Give."

"You all agree that travel is good for everyone. But if your purpose is to democratize life-enhancing travel, then your customer tribe should reflect that."

"And?" said David.

"It doesn't."

Silence.

"I see what you're saying," said David, pointing to the poster on the wall. "If we really want to democratize travel the way our purpose statement says, we'll need to recruit a lot more non-white, non-college-educated, blue-collar people to our brand. We can't be satisfied with the customers we already have."

Shigeru grinned. He went over and shook David's hand. "I was hoping someone would say that," said Shigeru. "Your purpose statement is already making demands on your strategy. It's saying you need to be more inclusive."

"What do you mean, 'more inclusive?'" said Steve.

Shigeru nodded toward David.

"More black and brown people," he said. "More people outside cities. More people who haven't traveled as much as they might like to. We've already signed up a lot of the easy-to-get customers. We have to figure out how to widen the circle."

"Not so fast," said Cary. "Are we sure that non-white, non-college-educated, blue-collar people are interested in eco-travel? Or is that an assumption? Where are you getting this?"

David was quickly developing a dislike for researchers. "From experience with consumers. What are you saying?"

"That you might be imposing your personal beliefs on those consumers. You know—that travel is good for people. That the world wants us to democratize travel. That eco-hotels are life-enhancing. But for whom? When? In what circumstances? These are questions I'd like to explore before we get too far."

Her questions felt like tiny darts. David folded his arms.

Shigeru went to the whiteboard. "Assuming we can vet those assumptions, this is our challenge in the simplest possible terms." He drew a circle with the letter *A* inside it. To the right of that, he drew a bigger circle with the letter *B*. "We know we can't just enlarge circle *A*. We have to find a path from *A* to *B*—from our current state to a better one."

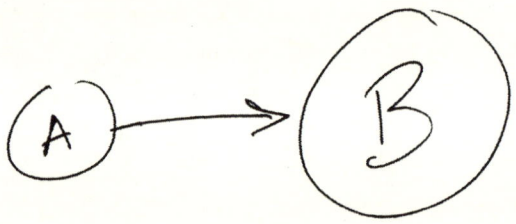

He drew a horizontal arrow between the two. "To get from *A* to *B*, we'll need a clear mission and vision."

"Should we do another exercise?" said Talia.

"Not quite yet. Let's think about our tribe. Our brand has to be about them, like we said. What's the highest good we can bring to our customers?"

A few people gave the ceiling another go-around.

"Well, we could open the door to a bigger world," said Yasemin. Several people nodded vigorously.

"Why is that a good thing?" said Shigeru.

"Because...I'm not sure why."

Michael came to the rescue. "Because, Yaz, one becomes a bigger person. One's knowledge, understanding, and zest for life increase dramatically."

Shigeru looked around the room. "How does that square with your purpose?"

Yaz smiled. The others nodded their approval. The team members buzzed with confidence as Gard dismissed them for the day.

David, however, was beginning to have his doubts.

15

BATTLEGROUND

Wednesday, December 15. As the Prius joined the northward flow of yellow cabs, David tried to formulate his question.

"Hey, Sok."

"Yeah?

"Ever travel?"

His eyes appeared in the mirror. "Sure. Harlem to Wall Street, Bowery to the Bronx, Midtown to the airport."

"I mean, do you ever travel *from* the airport."

"Listen, I'm an Uber driver. I make like a dollar-fifty an hour. My wife has to work so I can go to night school. We can barely keep our two kids in clothes. Travel is not an option."

"But you do dream of it."

He shrugged. "Sure, we dream of it. More for the girls than ourselves. Someday we'd like to take them to Greece, maybe a few other places: Paris, London, the usual."

"How about the kids you grew up with? The kids in the gangs, the kids hiding from gangs."

"I doubt it. Traveling for pleasure is for rich people. If gang-bangers had that much money, they'd probably buy guns," he said. "Why?"

David gazed out the window. "Just wondered."

The low winter sun slanted brightly through the crosstown

streets. But all he could see were the shadows, dismal and dark, as if the buildings were winning against the sky.

Early that morning he'd called Andy to give him an update on the team's progress. He tried to keep it positive, but the truth was they didn't have much to show for their efforts. Not yet, anyway. Andy was silent as David recapped their work on the purpose statement and customer profile. He had hoped it would resonate, but if it did, Andy gave no sign. All he said was, "Okay, see you Wednesday."

Wednesday's checkpoint meeting with the board was a week away. He needed to assure the members that things were moving in the right direction—he wasn't certain they were. The team had found a starting point, true, but nothing resembling a breakthrough.

Cary taped printouts of the previous day's work on the wall, while David and the others poured coffees and fixed their bagels. She'd pared the statements down to a few strong, clear sentences. Gard asked the team members to take their seats, and then turned the meeting over to Shigeru.

"Morning, everyone. On Monday we answered the first of the five strategy questions: What's our purpose?" He walked over to the poster and tapped the statement. "Yesterday we made a start on the second question: Who do we serve?" He gestured toward the poster describing BigSky's customers. "And today we'll tackle question number three: Where should we compete?"

Steve was losing patience. "If this is about which business we're in, isn't it obvious? We're in the fucking hotel business. I know you guys have your process, but can't we just check that box and move on?"

The members traded anxious glances, not sure how to respond to this sudden outburst. David sat with his face buried in cupped hands. He finally raised his head and turned toward Steve.

"Let's let Shig take us through the exercise and see what happens. We know we're in the hotel business, but we also know if we don't do something different, we won't be able to save the company. Shig, please continue."

"Steve's right," said Shigeru. "We *are* in the hotel business. The problem is the hotel business is suffering—and may not recover soon. We may need to pick a different battle, one we can win. For instance, maybe explore a different part of the hotel business or modify our offering to work around problems we have little power to change. Let's break into our teams for forty-five minutes. Try to define our business in a way that gives us the maximum scope for achieving our purpose. Any questions?"

There were no questions, but David could see the group was starting to feel some of the frustration that Gard had warned about. Yet, like good soldiers, they hunkered down.

"That was hard," announced Talia when they reconvened. She reported on her own team's conversation. They'd had trouble coming up with anything new. BigSky was in the hotel business, of course, but it was actually in two subcategories of the industry, eco-lodges and airport hotels. Moreover, the company could claim to be in a subcategory of a subcategory, since the Sojourners were unique among airport hotels—at least so far. How could they change their business? All they could think of was to sell off some of the international properties and increase the number of domestic eco-lodges. At least these would require less arduous travel for their customers.

David's team was only slightly more successful, wondering if the answer might lie in the airport business. What if the Sojourner model could be expanded outside the airports? Fifty years earlier, Motel 6 had disrupted the hotel industry with its no-frills $6 rooms, the equivalent—in today's dollars—of Sojourner's $48 rooms. The scope for expansion might be sizable.

Michael recapped his own team's progress, which was "bollocks" in his considered opinion. Steve thought they might be able to make up the revenue shortfall by attracting wealthier people to the eco-lodges. If they adopted industry best practices—luxury spas and helicopter shuttles, for example—they could command higher room rates and rack up fatter profits.

Shigeru thanked the teams for their presentations and looked around the room. "What do we think of these ideas in light of our purpose statement and customer profile?"

"They suck like a Dyson," Michael said. "Admit it, every one of these is a betrayal of our core principles. The first team wants to build a wall around our growth, shrinking our ambitions and reneging on our vow to help ordinary people expand their horizons.

"My own team," he said, narrowing his eyes at Steve, "would happily dump our promise to democratize travel, excluding the very people we want to help.

"Team three would undoubtedly succeed with their Motel 6 model. But to what advantage? It wouldn't be long before every hotel chain in the country was racing to catch up, leaving us gasping for breath while our eco-lodges died a slow death."

There was an awkward second of silence—then the room blew up. The finger-pointing began. Offended parties fought back vociferously, launching counterattacks with abandon. Michael blamed Steve for breaking the spirit of the employees. Steve blamed Yasemin for increasing cleaning time with her room layouts. Yasemin blamed Raven for raiding the design budget to pay for partnership programs.

David leaned toward Yasemin. "Raven isn't here, Yaz. We shouldn't talk behind her back." Yasemin's cheeks flushed. He turned to the group and clapped his hands. "Hey, everybody, cool it. None of us here is the enemy." He appealed to Shigeru for assistance.

Battleground

Shigeru stood up and waited for the steam to evaporate. When everyone settled down, he held up his phone to show the time. "It's past noon, folks. Why don't we take a nice, long lunch and meet back here at two. Sound good?"

David huddled with Gard over cafeteria pasta, voicing his concern that the participants were becoming polarized. He'd seen it happen in other companies, when the pressure of deadlines, budgets, and job insecurity created divisions instead of solidarity.

Gard went over to talk to Shigeru. The two of them returned to the conference room just as everyone else filtered back in.

Shigeru tapped on a water glass with his pen to get their attention. "Welcome back, everyone. What David said before lunch about enemies reminded me of something. Sometimes, when you identify your number-one enemy, the battlefield becomes more obvious. So who *is* our enemy?"

The participants looked at each other, unsure about the intent of the question.

"You mean our top competitor?" said Talia. "It's hard to say, since we don't go head to head with anybody. We compete with companies like Natura and FourWinds on location, but not on price. We compete with Ecco and Logix on price, but not on design. We compete on design with Summerland and Beau Voyage, but not on location. None of these can match our combination of location, price, and design."

"What about Sojourner?" said Shigeru.

"There's nothing like it on the market," said Yasemin. "No one has figured out how to win with a $48 price tag."

"So how do you do it?"

"We use design. In every possible way. From the hotels and rooms to the manufacturing and operational systems."

"Result: No competition?"

"Not yet—knock on reclaimed barn wood," she said, rapping her knuckles on the worktable.

"Okay, no direct competition on the eco-lodge side, and no competition *period* on the gotel side. Is that right? There must be an enemy. There's always an enemy if you look hard enough." Shigeru waited for volunteers.

Michael slid his chair back abruptly and strode over to the window. He threw open the blinds. The afternoon sun bounced a harsh light off the shimmering gold walls across the street. They squinted against the glare, their faces yellow-green from the reflected rays. The letters B-U-L-L seemed to loom larger and uglier than ever.

"*That's* the enemy," said Michael, pointing. "Not the man. Not the company. The crassness behind it. Bad taste on a biblical scale. This isn't just a lack of sophistication. It's a moral deficiency born of dishonesty, selfishness, egotism, and ruthlessness. *That's* our enemy. *That's* the battlefield. I say 'Cry havoc, and let slip the dogs of war!'"

The room erupted into argument for the second time. Michael had tossed a grenade that sent ideological shrapnel in every direction. Some of the members jumped up to confront him. David slumped in his chair, eyes closed, head slowly turning from side to side. He took a breath and rose to his feet.

"People," he said, clapping his hands loudly. "*People*!" The din began to attenuate. A few members took their seats. Others remained standing.

"I appreciate your anger and frustration. The situation is difficult. But we can't simply take the easy way out and blame our problems on the situation. Politics is not in our control. We can only hit the ball where it's pitched."

Steve threw his pen on the table. "Baseball metaphors are all fine and good," he said. "But our jobs are on the line here. The only way out of this mess is to get tough: we have to bear down, cut costs, and trim the workforce. This strategic mumbo jumbo is a colossal waste of time."

David turned to Gard and silently mouthed the word *help*.

Gard stood up. "It's been a long day, everyone. There's truth in what Steve says, but I think we need to work through the five Qs to find the right solution. We can start again in the morning when we're refreshed."

David rose to join Gard at the front. He turned to face the group. "Tonight, while you're having your glass of wine, I'd like you think about how we can work together without taking sides. The enemy might be out there," he said, gesturing toward the window. "Or it might be in here," he said, tapping his forehead. "But it's not the person sitting across the table from you."

He looked over and noticed Cary standing against the wall, eyes locked on his. The others had closed their laptops in preparation to leave.

Yasemin shouted over the sound of shuffling papers.

"Steve, did you forget something?"

He spun, a puzzled look on his face.

She held out his wallet. "I thought you might need this. You know, for the next time you feel like buying me a drink."

He clutched instinctively at his empty coat pocket. "How did you get that?" he said, more surprised than angry.

"Child's play," she said. The room dissolved into laughter, the rage and frustration dissipating under the spell of Yasemin's timely sleight of hand.

He smiled broadly and walked over, cupping her elbow as he walked her to the door. "There's a good bar down the street, Yasemin dear. Just promise me you'll keep your hands to yourself."

Cary had vanished along with Gard and Shigeru. David felt a

judder and grabbed his phone. A message had just come in from Raven. She'd be back in time for tomorrow's session.

If anything, his sense of anxiety deepened.

16

FIVE Ps

Thursday, December 16. David gave up trying to sleep and reached over to the nightstand to check the time: *4:26 a.m.* It could be worse. He'd probably managed to get in a few winks. He made the bed, showered, dressed, and went downstairs to the kitchen.

He knew Raven's return would throw the whole effort into sharp relief. She was well aware of the problems at BigSky—she'd seen her numbers dropping for a year. But she didn't know about the meeting with Andy, the ultimatum from the board, or the final presentation, now only twenty days away. He'd already decided not to bother the team about the checkpoint meeting next Wednesday.

But Gard was right—Raven needed to be involved in the strategy. *Revenue* is the *R* in CRO, a job title she took seriously. The problem was she became defensive and dismissive whenever the subject of revenues came up.

Raven was always competitive. She grew up in the South, a steel magnolia from Atlanta. She got through college on a track scholarship, accustomed to winning firsts in sprints, middle-distance, hurdles, and relay races. She hadn't stopped racing since then. She joined the Marriott training program and quickly made it to regional VP before BigSky recruited her twelve years ago.

In retrospect, her trip to Fiji had been a fool's errand. One

Five Ps

more eco-lodge, no matter how remarkable, would not reverse BigSky's sliding sales. And with US-Asia travel routes set to close, it might be years before Fiji became a viable option again.

David felt guilty that he hadn't brought her back earlier, but, in truth, he was overwhelmed by the situation and didn't see how Raven could help. As chief revenue officer, she'd simply advocate for expanding the promotional budget and discounting the room rates. These changes would lead to lower margins, which in turn would lead to lower service standards. Over time, lower standards would cause lower occupancy rates or lower average rates, or both. A downward spiral if ever there was one.

He ached for a sympathetic ear. He texted Sokrates at six o'clock and quickly got a return text: *CU@7*. He filled the intervening hour by reading the *Wall Street Journal*. The news, as usual, was discouraging. Thanks to knee-jerk trade restrictions and the growing threat of war, economists were now projecting a full-on recession by August.

"Long time no hear from," said Sokrates, as David climbed into the back seat. "Me worried. Chief okay?"

David laughed and shook his head at this lapse in political correctness. "Brave no worry."

He knew what his management professor would say about sharing information with outsiders: "Loose lips sink ships." But the more he opened up to Sokrates, the more trust he felt. He told him about the progress on the five *Q*s, including the purpose statement and customer profile. He described the team's differences on where to compete—whether to focus on domestic eco-lodges, extend the gotels beyond airports, or move the lodge business up to the luxury category. He also described the food fight over who the real enemy was, and the team's tendency to blame the situation instead of getting down to work.

Sokrates slowly nodded. "It sounds like the problem is you don't know what the problem is."

David sat there, not quite comprehending.

"You can't decide whether it's a resource problem, a positioning problem, a customer problem, or an employee problem. All you know is your business doesn't align with your purpose. How can you solve a problem if you don't know what it is?"

"Sok," said David, clapping him on the shoulder. "You're a genius."

Gard was the first of the Cultura team to show up. David expressed his worry about their lack of progress. Was it possible that they hadn't defined the problem well enough? Gard had wondered the same thing. He asked Shigeru to downshift on the question of where the company should play.

The other participants arrived in ones and twos, bringing their breakfast goodies to the tables. Raven had sent an email saying she would take a cab from JFK as soon as she landed.

Shigeru walked to the head of the room. "Thanks for being on time, everyone. You'll probably agree that yesterday was a tough one. Today we're going to take another approach to the third Q, the question of where to compete."

He picked up a marker. "I'm going to share a set of tools called *design thinking*. Anyone know what that is?"

"Thinking about design?" offered Talia.

"Nope. Anyone else?"

"Thinking like a designer?" said Yasemin.

"Getting warmer."

"Thinking by making," said Michael. "Working through problems with prototypes."

Shigeru touched his finger to the tip of his nose. "Ding-ding-

ding! But before we can start, we need to know what problem we're solving. On Monday, I showed you the five *Q*s of strategy. Now I'll show you the five *P*s of design thinking."

He turned to the whiteboard and started writing:

1. Problemizing
2. Pinballing
3. Probing
4. Prototyping
5. Proofing

"These are the main components," he said. "So let's start with *problemizing*. Companies do fairly well with problem *solving*. But the real power lies in problem *framing*. Is this the right problem to solve? Is there a bigger problem lurking behind this one? Is the problem relevant? What other problems could we solve that would bring even more value to our customers?"

He handed a sheaf of exercise sheets to Cary, who passed them around to the teams. "I'm going to ask you to write a problem statement. As you can see, it's divided into three parts: the problem itself, the benefit of solving it, and opportunity cost—the cost of not solving it. Work in your teams for forty-five minutes, then come back and present to the group."

After the exercise Cary led the teams back into the room. She taped a large sheet to the whiteboard.

"I consulted the Market Penetration Index to compare BigSky's occupancy with the market average. BigSky is actually doing better than its competitors, which seems to confirm our initial hunch that the problem is not us, but the industry.

"Based on that, the output of the three teams came out pretty much the same. It was easy to combine the output of all three teams into a single problem statement. Tell me if I've captured your ideas fairly. If not, please keep your lousy opinions to yourself."

A few members snickered.

"You can see why they don't let me lead the workshops." Turning toward the whiteboard, she read her combined statement:

> *Problem:*
> *The hotel industry has experienced a serious downturn across all categories. Fears of terrorism, the spread of xenophobia, and draconian security procedures have dampened the public's desire for travel.*
>
> *Solution benefit:*
> *With the right solution, we can either help to reverse these trends or work around them, thereby getting our business back on track.*
>
> *Opportunity cost:*
> *If we do too little or nothing at all, we'll continue on a downward spiral of disappearing customers, falling revenues, and shrinking profits, eventually leading to the sale of our assets. Thousands of people could lose their jobs.*

Silence. Then somebody spoke from the back of the room. "I'd say you've captured the problem perfectly." A tall woman in a gray suit stood by the rear door, a metallic gray rollaboard at her side. Her hair was black with silver threads running through it—Raven.

"Welcome home, stranger," said David, jumping up to grab her hand. "Come in and meet the folks from Cultura." He introduced her to Gard, Shigeru, and Cary. He gave her a brief tour of the output from the first three days. Then he said to the group,

"Excuse us for a second." He led her out to the hallway.

"There's something I need to tell you," he said in a low voice verging on monotone. He brought her up to speed on the board's sudden ultimatum and the looming deadline. Raven was ten years older than David and had always made him feel like a schoolboy in the principal's office.

She looked straight at him. "How long have you known this?"

"Raven, I'm sorry. I didn't want to interrupt your trip. I figured it could wait until you got back."

"You figured it could wait. I'm furious. How many days until the presentation?"

"Twenty. Nineteen after today."

"And what happens if the board doesn't like your plan?"

"Our plan," he corrected her. "We're doing this together. They have to like it. We have no choice. I need you to pitch in and help us crack the problem."

"I can't believe you left me in Fiji, knowing all the while there was no way the deal would happen."

"I'm sorry. I wasn't thinking. You must be exhausted after your flight. Please go home and get some rest. Can you join us tomorrow at nine?"

"Oh. I'll be here."

17

PINBALL

Friday, December 17. Shigeru glanced around. The group assembled into its teams, five per table. Raven found a seat with Steve, Talia, Gard, and Yasemin. Her face showed a fierce determination.

David glanced at Gard. Gard nodded as if to say, "Don't worry, I've got this."

"Today," said Shigeru, "we'll pool our imagination to pry open some tough problems, including the overall problem outlined in our statement. But first I want to tell you a story."

Several team members leaned forward. Steve sat back and folded his arms.

"My wife and I live in the suburbs," Shigeru started. "Last summer a hummingbird got into our house. The weather was warm, and we'd left the back door open. Certain birds are programmed to fly upward whenever they get in trouble. Nine times out of ten this instinct will take them to safety. The hummingbird had flown to the top of our cathedral ceiling, where it was frantically bumping against the beams. We opened the doors and windows and turned off the lights, but the little creature kept charging the ceiling."

"What happened?" asked Yasemin.

"Hummingbirds can only go so long without refueling. Eventually the poor thing ran out of gas and fell to the floor, exhausted. My wife picked it up and set it on a table outside. It lay there, face down, wings out, frozen with shock and fatigue. After a few minutes, the tiny bird revived and flew straight to the top of a tree." Shigeru looked around at the group and waited.

"And the moral is?" said Talia.

"The moral is," said Shigeru, "if you want to innovate, you need to escape your programming. Sometimes you need to fly sideways, or even downward, before you can get unstuck. You can't always fly straight up and out."

Heads nodded.

"And what does that mean for us BigSky birds?" said Steve.

"It means we have to apply our imagination to solve intractable problems."

Pinball

Raven said, "We can imagine all we want, but that doesn't mean we'll succeed. There's nothing new under the sun, right? Why can't we just use best practices like everyone else? We'd be idiots not to find out how other people have solved the same problem. Copy and paste. They've already done the hard work and taken the risk."

Shigeru looked around. "Thoughts, anyone?"

"I think what Shig is saying," said David, "is that we're in a unique situation that can't be addressed with an off-the-shelf solution. We're in new territory where best practices don't apply."

"We just haven't tried hard enough," said Raven, shaking her head. "The answer is pretty straightforward—funnel all our resources into sales until we get back on track."

David started to speak, but paused to consider Shigeru's lesson. *Some birds are programmed to fly upward whenever they get in trouble.*

"You might be right, Raven," he finally said. "But let's see if we can put some new ideas on the table. Then we can choose from a wider range of options. We don't want to make the mistake of throwing good money after bad." He regretted the words as soon they left his mouth.

"Oh, I see—it's bad money if we spend it on *my* department."

"That's not what I mean. Listen, Raven, you're amazing. An absolute rock. Nobody works harder than you do, and we'll support you with every resource we have."

She calmed down, her feathers smoothed.

"Why don't we let Shig take us through the exercises and see what happens?" He looked to Shigeru for help. Yasemin sketched a small dead bird, lying upside down with its feet curled.

"Okay," said Shigeru. "Has anyone played pinball?" Most of the participants raised their hands. "Can you visualize the machine? The bumpers, bells, and blinking lights? The second *P* of design thinking is called *pinballing*. By using specific techniques, we can get our ideas to bounce off each other like the silver balls in a pinball machine, producing new directions we could never imagine with routine logic. Let me share three of these techniques.

"The first is *reversing assumptions*. You start by making a list of all the things people believe about your industry. For example, most people believe that eco-hotels are designed for vacations; that only adventurous people travel long distances; and that foreign countries pose dangers. You might flip these assumptions by saying eco-hotels are for not for vacations; that timid people like to travel long distances; and that foreign countries are the safest places in the world. Then you could think about what would have to change to make this second set of assumptions true. When you start from a reversed position, it's nearly impossible to end up in the same rut.

"The second technique is *arranging blind dates*. A blind date is when you introduce two ideas that have never met before. To improve the eco-hotel model, for example, you might think of something random—let's say a toaster. How could a toaster improve a hotel? Well, maybe every room has a sun lamp, so even if the weather is bad, guests still come home with a tan. Just like toast, they pop up nice and brown."

Laughter coursed through the room.

"Okay, probably not a game changer," he said sheepishly. "The third technique is *thinking in metaphors*. The idea here is to imagine how something might be similar to something else. Metaphors act as catalysts to change one reality into another.

"For example, what if you said that an eco-hotel was like a cruise ship? In that case, maybe all the guests would board at the same time. Maybe they'd go through the same one- or two-week experience together. The activities might be planned, like a menu, including games, meals, and entertainment. Viewing a hotel through the metaphor of a cruise ship could change everything and bring you into a whole new market space.

"Let's break into our teams and see what we can do. Use any of these techniques you like. We'll meet back here in an hour to share our thoughts."

The group returned with their exercise sheets in hand, chatting excitedly. Shigeru asked for volunteers.

Yasemin stood up and said that her team had luck with the blind date technique, combining an eco-hotel with a natural history museum. Guests would go on hikes wearing headphones. A recorded audio guide would direct them to the most interesting sights, explaining the history and ecology behind each one. They'd get a souvenir booklet for each excursion they took, and their photos could be snapped at various landmarks and made available for purchase at the end of the tour. The hotel stores would serve as museum shops, increasing revenues per customer as they loaded up on well-designed souvenirs.

The GM for the eco-lodges spoke for her team. They had flipped a number of assumptions and come up with several new ideas. Instead of cleaning the rooms every day, as in a typical hotel, rooms would only be cleaned on weekends. Guests would stay in one-week increments, coming and going on Saturdays. The eco-lodges could offer much lower nightly rates by organizing the stays and limiting the work of the cleaning staff to a single day each week. Lower prices would bring more business.

When the once-a-week cleaning concept was suggested, Cary's face puckered. David glanced over and Cary instantly changed her sour expression to a delighted one, as if to say, "Mmm, what a lovely idea."

Michael said his team had tried to think in metaphors, imagining the eco-hotels as schools. They would enroll people from all over the world in localized environmental studies. Each hotel would have its own teaching staff: specially trained guides who would take their students into the field and explain the natural wonders of the area. The hotels would partner with colleges and universities to create classes for credits. Each student would receive a certificate.

"Okay, these are great," said Shigeru.

Steve shook his head. "Schools don't make any money," he said flatly. "We'd end up much worse off than we are now."

"You're probably right," said Shigeru. "But innovation doesn't end with the first idea. You have to coddle it, feed it, nurture it into something more. New ideas are like babies. They're fragile. You have to protect them while they develop."

"Well, these babies are pretty stupid."

David interrupted. "Easy, Steve. We're just starting to get some momentum."

"If you say so. But I happen to believe Raven is right. We should cut costs and pour the savings into promotions. We'd have the train back on track in no time. All this brainstorming is ridiculous. It's wasteful. We're taking all these people off line when we could be fixing the company."

"Gee, Steve," said Michael. "Tell us what you really think."

David rose quickly and went to the front of the room. "Okay, everyone. It's nearly six. We've had a long week. We're tired. I think we're making great headway. Let's all go home and have a nice relaxing weekend, and meet back here on Monday morning."

David wasn't tired, though. He was fuming.

18

COOPERSTOWN

Saturday, December 18. Another sleepless night. Questions swam endless laps in David's head. Was he angry with Steve and Raven for their stubborn insistence on short-term solutions? Or was he angry with himself for believing he could reinvent the wheel?

The team had certainly proposed a wide range of options: email campaigns, seasonal discounts, national advertising, branded products, sponsored entertainment, celebrity-designed eco-lodges. Then there were the structural possibilities of extending the gotel franchise, expanding the eco-lodges domestically, and partnering with retailers to create special programs. There were also brute-force remedies such as channeling more of the budget into sales and selling off properties to raise cash.

Despite the doubts raised by Steve and Raven, Cultura's strategy process was beginning to feel powerful—a locomotive steadily gathering steam. It was a far cry from the flailing, hit-and-miss brainstorming of the strategy team's earlier efforts. Now they had a muscular purpose statement, a clear picture of who their customers were, and a well-defined problem to solve. True, the members had faltered on the third Q of where to compete, but the five Ps of design thinking had already produced a step change in the quality of their ideas. Further exercises would produce even better results.

The upcoming Wednesday meeting hung over David's head like the sword of Damocles. He couldn't go to the board with the work the team had completed so far—he'd have to answer that third strategy question. There were only two more sessions before the meeting to make the where-to-compete answer come into focus. His mind was a dizzying whirl. He needed to slow it down.

If there was one thing he'd learned as an architect, it was the power of the creative prelude. Every brainiac from Aristotle to Einstein has extolled the merits of *incubation*, the period between absorbing a problem and finding its solution. It might take five minutes in the shower. Or an hour's walk in the woods. Some of the greatest artists and scientists hit upon remarkable ideas after spending a few weeks on vacation, doing nothing. During these quiet periods the logical mind lays fallow, allowing the subconscious to work behind the scenes to produce a sudden flash of insight. Worth a try. No flashes had been forthcoming from *this* mind for quite a while.

He brought his café au lait to the dining table and opened his laptop. He typed in *Cooperstown*. Up came the National Baseball Hall of Fame and Museum. It was odd, he thought, that after all these years of trying to bury his past, he now seemed drawn to it. He'd always dreamed of visiting the Hall of Fame. In fact, he'd once dreamed of being *in* it. A childhood fantasy, for sure, but dreams have a way of shaping people's lives. You ignore them at your peril.

The map on the museum website showed Cooperstown as a lakeside village in upstate New York, about 200 miles north of the city. He decided to spend the weekend among the bronze plaques and arcane memorabilia of baseball's greatest heroes.

He could ask Jan in corporate travel to arrange a flight and hotel for him, but he wasn't in a social mood. All he wanted was a relaxing weekend on his own to bathe in the quaint ephemera of his boyhood pursuit. An online search showed that the airport closest to Cooperstown was Oneonta, but it seemed liked a municipal field that catered to private and charter planes. The two next-closest airports, Albany and Syracuse, were each an hour-and-a-half away. He could hire a car or take a bus from either city to Cooperstown.

He logged onto a booking site. There was a flight to Albany

from LaGuardia, but it detoured south through Philadelphia, making the total flight almost five hours. The flight he found to Syracuse detoured farther south to Washington and would take even longer.

JFK had better options, although the airport was a schlep from his apartment. There was a flight to Albany with a stop in Washington that would get him there in just under four hours. A little more research uncovered a non-stop flight on JetBlue that would get him there in less than two hours. Good old JetBlue. He quickly entered his information. Too late—no seats available.

There must be a train.

Amtrak listed a route that went as far as Utica, departing from nearby Penn Station. He could grab a taxi to the station, take the train to Utica, and catch a bus to Cooperstown. Total travel time? Seven hours. His heart sank. Seven hours to cover 200 miles.

He could rent a car, of course, but he was looking forward to reclaiming the sleep he'd been cheated out of during the past week. He checked the Greyhound schedule online. He knew that most Americans viewed buses as second-class transportation. But the rest of the world, including David, viewed them as perfectly respectable modes of travel. They're not only quiet and comfortable, but the drivers will often drop you along the route if you ask politely.

Here it was. Penn Station to Kingston, then Kingston to Cooperstown. Travel time: five-and-a-half hours. Better than seven hours on the train. Just then a small notice popped onto the screen—in the winter months, the bus to Cooperstown didn't run on Saturdays.

Okay. It would have to be Amtrak. He'd arrive in the evening, tour the museum first thing in the morning, and take the same route back in the afternoon. He booked the tickets, and reserved a room at a nice-looking B & B called The Inn at Cooperstown.

He packed an overnight bag and got himself to the station.

The minute he took his seat on the train, he fell into a well-earned coma.

19

EPIPHANY

Sunday, December 19. The pure December sun fell on David's shoulders as he trotted up the steps of the museum. Inside, the place was deserted except for a young father and his two boys.

David paid the entrance fee and took a brochure. The text on the back said the museum was built in 1939 by a Scot named Alexander Cleland, who got the idea after watching workers expand nearby Doubleday Field. The ground floor housed the Hall of Fame, a gallery of bronze plaques honoring the game's all-time greats.

It took David less than a minute to find his hero, Nolan Ryan. Ryan had paired his lightning fastball with a devastating curve, a one-two combination that racked up a career record of 5,714 strikeouts. His pitches often clocked in at 100 miles an hour.

Down the hall was Babe Ruth, the "Sultan of Swat." Ruth started as a pitcher, but was too valuable as a hitter to play only once every three or four games.

Not too far from Ruth was Willie Mays, the "Say Hey Kid." Some believe he was the greatest player of all time. His acrobatic catch in the 1954 World Series was the stuff of legend.

Further down the hall was pitcher Cy Young. Young held the record for both career wins *and* losses.

And here was Lou Gehrig, who in 1939 gave the deadly disease ALS its nickname. He'd played 2,130 games without ever calling in sick.

Epiphany

David turned and saw Ted Williams, baseball's last .400 hitter. Williams used his Hall of Fame induction speech to insist that Satchel Paige and Josh Gibson—two black players who had been barred from major league baseball—should be in the Hall of Fame. David thought about his company's new purpose: to make travel possible for everyone. Could BigSky become the Ted Williams of travel?

David learned about Henry Chadwick, not a player but a statistician. Before 1900, he invented metrics that are still in use today—the batting average, the earned-run average, the box score, and the numbering of field positions.

A century later came Bill James. He took statistics to a whole new level with sabermetrics, the analysis of why teams win and lose. The term *sabermetrics* comes from the acronym SABR, the Society for American Baseball Research. With the introduction of these new metrics, baseball managers and die-hard fans could now predict a team's performance with more accuracy—or at least informed superstition. Branch Rickey, the pioneering executive who hired the first black and Latino players, helped bring sabermetrics into the front office. Rickey was in the Hall of Fame, whereas James was not.

David spent the remainder of the morning strolling through the museum, admiring old uniforms and quaint memorabilia. Here, the first glove with webbing between the thumb and forefinger ("designed by pitcher Bill Doak and made by Rawlings Sporting Goods"); there, a leather baseball with broken stitching ("The Babe knocked the cover off of that one!"); and next to that, a massive collection of old baseball cards—the first ones appeared in the 1860s in cigarette packages.

As the morning progressed, the museum came alive with visitors. A pleasant hum filled the hallways and galleries. It reminded David of the minutes before a game, the excitement that spectators feel as they bring their popcorn to the bleachers, the bright sun intensifying the greens of the grass and the crisp white lines of the infield.

The sound of raised voices broke his reverie—the two boys from earlier in the morning.

"You hold it like this," said the older boy. They were arguing in front of an exhibit on baseball grips.

"Gimme that," said the younger one, grabbing the ball from his brother's hand. "It's like this!" Nearby adults had been shushing them for the last few minutes. The boys paid little attention.

As David approached, they stopped and looked up. His six feet two towered over their four feet something. He sat on his haunches and held out his hand. The younger boy placed the ball in it. "I used to be a professional pitcher. What do you want to know?"

They looked at each other with a mixture of fear and awe. The younger one spoke first: "He says you throw a curveball like this." He took the ball and made a twisting motion with his hand.

"Okay," said David. "First of all, you're gripping it wrong. Make sure your middle finger runs along the inside of a seam, like this," he said, demonstrating with the ball. "You know how to throw a ninety-mile-an-hour fastball?"

"Sure," said the younger boy.

"A curve is different. With the fastball, you bring your arm forward, in the direction of the plate. With a curve, you bring your arm down to get rotation. You hook your hand just a little as you throw, letting your middle finger spin the ball. If you twist your hand too much, your curve will be too slow. If you don't hook it at all, it won't have any movement. You want about thirteen revolutions between your hand and home plate."

They looked skeptical. The older one said, "How can you tell if there's thirteen revolutions?"

"You can't. But you'll know, because the batter will look like a complete fool. You'll say to yourself, 'Thirteen revolutions—nailed it.' But don't use it too much. Only when you feel like giving the batter the middle finger."

They howled with glee. David slapped the ball into the younger boy's hand. They took off down the hall, laughing, looking for Dad.

David's phone buzzed and chimed. He reached into his pocket: *12:30*. Just enough time to catch the bus to Utica for the 2:25 train. He'd get back to Penn Station by 9:30 and be in bed by 10:00. A lot of traveling, for sure, but he had to admit that he'd never felt more energized.

The bus rolled smoothly through the bare winter countryside, passing the hamlets of Cattown, Schuyler Lake, and Dennison Corners. Just before Mohawk, it began to decelerate. Yellow detour signs appeared on the right side of the road. The driver announced a delay due to ongoing highway construction. David sighed. Shouldn't the passengers have been warned about this?

By the time they arrived at the Amtrak station, the 2:25 had already left. The man in the booth said no refunds, but another train would depart at 3:45. David bought a second ticket. This particular train would take nine hours instead of seven. He'd get home at one o'clock in the morning.

He leaned back in his seat as the 3:45 pulled out of the station twenty minutes late. Why is it so hard to travel such a short distance? If a weekend trip to Cooperstown is this complicated, what's it like for BigSky's customers, who sometimes have to travel thousands of miles to reach an eco-lodge? Undoubtedly, they were routinely subjected to multiple connections, long layovers, interminable security lines, iffy ground transportation. David had always been more focused on the hotels themselves—the design, the experience, the atmosphere, the service. He hadn't thought about the end-to-end experience.

The strategy team had been right about the travel business: it was in a slump, simple as that. Terrorism, inconvenience, and rising xenophobia had taken their toll on the industry. The *industry*. Not the company. *Why can't you just build a new business and let the others simmer for a while? It's not like you can fix the economy.*

Just like that, it hit him.

They'd been looking for a company solution, when they should have been looking for an *industry* solution. They couldn't change the business climate. But they could try to work with it. Use it. Solve the larger problem for their customers.

Better hotels or more hotels were not the answer. Nor were better marketing, pouring money into sales, cutting back employee hours, or selling off properties. People weren't traveling, period. *That* was the problem BigSky had to solve. Customers weren't looking for great hotels. They were looking for help in fulfilling their dreams. They were looking for life-enhancing experiences—the team's answer to the first *Q*. It was so obvious. How could he have missed it?

If the problem was travel itself, then they needed to fix travel. *How?* The behaviors of airports, airlines, and national politicians were not their department. What is it that travelers want? What is it that customers of any kind want?

They probably want a sense of control over their purchases. They want their buying decisions to be easy. They crave the emotional kick of making a smart, enjoyable investment in their lives. What they don't want are mistakes and unnecessary obstacles. The more complex life becomes, the more they yearn for simplicity. How could BigSky simplify travel?

In an earlier time, the problem of planning a journey must have been fairly complicated. How did people solve it? They handed it to a travel agent. The travel agent had access to brochures, timetables, and current prices, as well as firsthand experience with popular destinations.

Since then, the body of knowledge about travel had grown exponentially. Today, no single head can hold that much information. And so the job of "travel agent" has been *disintermediated*—a Silicon Valley term for removing the middle man through technology. Now there are websites for choosing and booking hotels, flights, rail travel, and rental cars without third-party assistance. Most of these include systems for customer rankings and reviews. Customers can read for themselves how other travelers fared.

Yet the process of travel today is far from simple. In fact, David realized, it's much more complicated now than it was in the era of travel agents. This was the problem the agents had been in business to solve. With the dying agency business, the tasks of piecing together a complex trip had fallen on the shoulders of customers.

A smile spread across David's face. There it was—the answer to the third Q, the question of where to compete.

They had to automate the agency business.

If BigSky could simplify travel using computing power, they'd not only help their hotel businesses, they'd create a new revenue stream in its own right, one that could not only *address* the complexity problem, but *thrive* on it.

David reached into his bag for his notebook and pen. They would need a website with a clear, intuitive interface. It needed to produce complete itineraries, not just suggestions for flights and hotels. This would no doubt require some kind of artificial intelligence on the back end. Maybe they could rent it. Or even design it themselves. They had to do for travel what sabermetrics had done for baseball.

Thoughts were flooding into his notebook. He'd filled a dozen pages with ideas when the train finally pulled in to Penn Station.

20

PROBING

Monday, December 20. In the morning, when the Cultura team showed up, David was already waiting in the *war room*, their new term for the conference room they'd commandeered. He pulled Gard aside and shared his epiphany from the day before. Could they possibly test his new idea with the group? Gard said the timing was perfect. They could move directly to the third *P*, *probing*, and take David's idea for a spin.

When the rest of the members settled in, Gard stood up to welcome them. "I hope you all had a relaxing weekend. On Friday we managed to get some radical ideas up on the walls." Six or seven large Post-it sheets testified to a significant burst of creativity. There were ideas for reframing the eco-lodges as living museums; lowering costs by organizing stays by the week instead of the night; and turning the lodges into educational partners for colleges and universities.

"We also heard a call for doubling down on sales and simply powering through the downturn," he said, nodding toward Raven and Steve. "Now, David would like to add one more idea to the mix."

A dozen heads turned. David walked to the front of the room. "I know, I know," he said. "We were supposed to take the weekend off. That's actually what I was doing—when I had an epiphany." They listened intently as he searched for the right words.

"It's as if we're trying to fix a tire," he said, "when the real problem is that the roads are closed. We're trying to save the eco-lodges by making them work harder. The deeper issue is that people aren't traveling. Which is exactly how we framed the problem. But then we switched to another one that was easier. We tried to change the tire instead."

Probing

He reminded everyone that the travel business was in a bind. Terrorism, inconvenience, xenophobia, and a growing recession had taken their toll on the industry. The team had been looking for a company solution, when it should have been looking for an industry solution.

"Are you saying all the work we've done was a waste of time?" said Talia, gesturing toward the cluttered walls.

"Not at all. But I think we should raise our game a notch." David related the story of his convoluted trip to Cooperstown—how there was no easy way to get there and no easy way to plan the journey.

"That's when it hit me. If we could solve *that* problem—the problem of planning complex trips to out-of-the-way places—we could offer a valuable service and solve our revenue problem at the same time. We can't change the xenophobic mood of the country, but we might make travel seem, I don't know, less forbidding."

"What's your idea?" said Michael, taking a sip of Perrier.

"To build an online travel agency."

"Pffffft!" Michael sprayed a mouthful of water across the table. The other members froze. Gasps punctuated the silence. Steve shook his head. "A travel agency. David, you've obviously been working too hard. You've lost your friggin' mind."

Yasemin said, "Wait—that's pretty good. We'd have a chance to build up our tribe and make a strong case for nature travel. We'd find out all kinds of things about our customers. Potential customers too." Before she could get another word in, the room erupted into animated discourse, opinion layered on opinion until all that could be heard were thrumming waves of white noise.

Gard got up and clapped his hands. "Team! *Team!*" When the racket finally subsided, he said, "It seems like David's idea has struck a chord in us. It might be a good idea. It may be truly bad. But it's got energy, and I think we should explore it." He walked over to a flip chart and took the top off a marker.

"This brings us to the third *P* of design thinking." He wrote P-R-O-B-I-N-G on the whiteboard. "What often happens to new ideas is that they're discarded before they can be developed. Or, conversely, they're adopted before they can be questioned. Groups are notorious for their inability to deliver great ideas. Tell me: what usually happens when a group comes up with a truly fresh, untried idea?"

"Someone attacks it," said Talia.

"Exactly. Human beings have been doing that to each other since the days of Plato. We call it 'having a discussion.' But it's more like having an argument. And while argument can sometimes help discern the true from the false, it rarely spawns new ideas. The world's inventions have usually happened in spite of argument, not because of it. Does anyone know where the word *discussion* comes from?"

"Latin," said Michael. "*Discutere*. To shake apart." He saw Talia make a pompous face and stick her nose in the air. "What?" he said.

"That's right, Michael," said Gard, "to shake apart. But innovators need to put things together, not shake them apart. It's about synthesis, not analysis. For my money, the best tool for synthesizing ideas in a group is *parallel thinking*."

"You mean that Edward de Bono stuff?" said Yasemin. "Six hats?"

"Yes! How many people know it?" said Gard. A few hands went up. "This De Bono guy was a fucking genius—shit, don't tell Heather. What I mean is, he was a truly bright man. A simplifier. In order to get around our natural Platonic tendencies, he came up with an approach called parallel thinking. Shig, do you want to explain?"

"Sure. The leader of a brainstorming session asks the whole group to think in the same direction at the same time. In other words, wear the same 'thinking hat.' Each hat represents one of six different directions. The white hat is for information, the red for emotion. The black hat is for caution, the yellow for positivity, the green for creativity. The blue hat is reserved for the facilitator, who determines which hat the group will wear at any given time. Shall we try it? I'll wear the blue hat." Shigeru reached into his bag and pulled out an L.A. Dodgers cap.

"Boooo," came the automatic response.

"Just kidding." He quickly replaced it with a New York Mets cap. "The rest of you can wear the white hat, the hat of information. Okay. What do we know about the travel agency business?"

"Nothing," said Steve. "That's the problem."

"So let's look at it from a customer's viewpoint. Anybody?"

"Agency services used to be free," said Talia. "At least for airline tickets. Now they charge for everything. That's been my experience, anyway."

Laptops flew open. David was first to report. "It says here on the ASTA website—American Society of Travel Agents—that the number of agencies charging fees has gone up from 61 percent to 91 percent in the last few years."

"Anything else?" said Shigeru.

Cary looked at her screen. "There are 100,000 travel agents in the US but the difficulty is finding one that fits your needs. The ASTA site offers a page of tips for locating the right agent. Sounds hard," she said, squinting at the small type.

"Well," said Raven, "they don't have much incentive to make travel easy, do they? And they're not likely to play favorites with their own members. The truth is organizations like to perpetuate the problems they're paid to solve."

Michael nodded, holding up an index finger. "It is difficult to get a man to understand something when his salary depends on his not understanding it."

"Shakespeare?" asked Talia.

"Upton Sinclair."

"Sounds like a Brit."

"A Yank—*duh*."

Talia gave him another look.

Shigeru continued to prod the white hats for more information, keeping pace with notes on the flip chart. After thirty minutes, he called for a change of direction.

"Let's try the red hat, the hat of emotion," he said. "Now that we know something about the travel agencies, let's say how we *feel* about the idea of building one for BigSky. David, at this point, I need to ask you if everyone has permission to be blunt."

"I think we can trust each other to be honest. I'd go even further. Our existence depends on it."

"Good. Let's take the temperature of the group. Steve, how do you feel about it?"

"I feel like it's a bad idea."

"Maybe you're not getting the concept of feeling. What's the *emotion* behind your belief that it's a bad idea?"

"I hate it."

Laughter rippled through the room. Steve was in his element. "I think it's an idiotic idea. We don't know the first thing about the travel agency business. Or about ecommerce, for that matter."

"All right, that's pretty blunt. But I'm going to stop you there. The whole idea of the red hat is to get the prevailing emotions out into the open so they don't come back disguised as logic. Emotions are just emotions. The reasons can come later. How about anyone else?"

One by one, they tried to pinpoint how they felt about David's idea. Under a *Red hat* heading, Shigeru did his best to capture the flood of words: scared, excited, cautious, cautiously optimistic, angry, confident, happy, hopeful, worried, intrigued, surprised, nervous, astonished.

Probing

"It looks like the *Attack of the Emoticons*," said David.

Cary rolled her eyes.

"Yep," said Shigeru. "We've got the full range here. Now let's explore the reasons for some of the more positive feelings. Take off the red hat and put on the yellow hat. The yellow hat stands for positivity. It gives us a chance to explore the kind of outcomes or benefits we'd love to see. Any ideas?"

Yasemin started off. "Users won't have to sift through dozens of hotels or airline choices to find the best one. The website would just *know*."

"You're dreaming, Yaz," said Steve. "Websites can't read minds."

"Steve," said Shigeru with quiet patience, "we're on the yellow hat. Dreaming is the whole point." Steve stuck his hands in his pockets and appeared to sulk.

"What would be really cool," said Yasemin, "is if the site could pump out complete, end-to-end itineraries instead of making users do all the work themselves."

"Maybe we could become the go-to website for bucket-list travel," added Talia.

Yellow-hat ideas began to flow. Shigeru used a kind of shorthand to keep up. He wrote *end 2 end* and *bkt list*.

"People could send their itineraries to friends."

"Itineraries could be free. People could create unlimited variations."

"Users would pay in one place for the whole trip—airline tickets, hotels, rental cars, everything."

David leaned back and smiled. The new brand was taking shape. Ideas tumbled one over the other.

"We could use customer info to send offers or even create new properties or future sub-brands based on their preferences."

"If we were the first to do this, we could pretty much own the market for it."

"We could build it as a standalone business and later spin it off."

When the flow of ideas finally stopped, Gard stood up and called for a recess. "It's past noon, folks. We agreed to work all day, so we'd better break for lunch. We'll meet back here in an hour. Try to get your emails and calls done before that. I'd like us to get through the rest of the hats by five tonight."

The mood was buoyant as the members filed down to the cafeteria. They pulled tables together and continued the conversation over pizza slices, salads, and vegetable pasta. Steve and Raven sat together on the far side of the room.

David sat with Shigeru. He'd become transfixed by Shig's ability to keep the group's thinking in a liquid state, instead of driving full speed at the obvious solution. He was beginning to see the outlines of a distinct philosophy.

"Tell me, Shig: How do you keep your mind open in the face of a deadline? Every fiber of my being wants to bring the strategy work to a close."

"Of course it does," he said. "The body and mind are uncomfortable with doubt. They try to banish it by grabbing at answers. I try to follow the example of Seng-ts'an."

"Who?"

"The third patriarch of Zen. Smart guy. He said, 'Do not seek the truth; only cease to cherish opinions.' He meant that you have to clear your mind of the desire for answers if you want to see what's there."

"Funny. That's almost identical to what a friend of mine said: 'Keep asking questions. Don't settle for easy answers'."

"Sounds like another smart guy."

Shigeru called the afternoon session to order. Raven immediately raised her hand.

"Raven?"

"Steve and I were talking," she said. "We heard some interesting ideas this morning, but most of them were—well, naïve. I don't mean to offend anyone—"

"That's a great point, Raven," said Shigeru. "Let's put on our black hats for the next session. The beauty of parallel thinking is that every point of view can be expressed without offending anyone. All perspectives are welcome under the appropriate hat.

"The black hat," he explained, "is the hat of caution, of warning, of rational fears. We human beings are exceptionally good at black-hatting. Our brains are hardwired to give more weight to danger than opportunity. If it weren't that way, we'd probably be extinct by now."

"Some people already are," quipped Michael, turning toward the building across the street. "They just don't know it yet."

"Now, Michael," said Gard in a finger-wagging tone. "You're talking about our president. Show some respect for the office."

"I thought we were on the black hat," said Michael.

Shigeru laughed and continued. "The black hat is the hat of the worst-case scenario."

"Precisely," said Michael.

"It's an early warning system for unworkable ideas. It tells you when you might need a Plan B." He looked around the room. "All right. Why do we think this whole website thing is doomed? Black hats, everyone."

Steve didn't miss a beat. "Because we have zero expertise and even less experience. The travel agency business might as well be the moon."

"Perfectly valid. Possibly a deal killer. Anyone else?"

"There's no obvious way to make money with it," said Raven.

"Good black-hat response."

"An experienced company like TripAdvisor," said Steve, "could blow by us without even breaking a sweat."

"And," said Raven, "trying to include all the world's destinations and all the world's travel options would take years, if not decades. We'd have to be another Google to pull that off."

David piled on. "And the legal exposure for botched itineraries could tie our business in knots. Imagine what would happen to our brand if people followed an itinerary and ended up seriously lost or got robbed after stumbling into the wrong part of town."

"On a slightly less dramatic but equally serious note," said Michael, "we could end up throwing thousands of travel agents out of work through disruption, the way Uber did to traditional taxi drivers."

"Hey, I like that idea," said Steve.

"Ah-*ah*," said Shigeru. "Black hat only, remember?"

"Okay," said Steve. "We're bound to fail because the website doesn't align with our hotel businesses. It makes more sense for somebody like TripAdvisor to do it. How's that?"

"Better."

Yasemin jumped in. "Customers would eventually resent us for putting our own interests ahead of theirs. How could we resist the temptation to showcase our own properties ahead of competitors?"

Shigeru filled five large sheets with black-hat objections.

Steve leaned back, hands laced behind his head, surveying the damage with satisfaction.

"Well done, black-hatters!" said Shigeru. "It looks pretty bad for David's idea. Now, let's swap our black hats for green ones. Green is the hat of creativity, imagination, and vision. Let's see if we can address some of these black-hat concerns with green-hat workarounds."

The group stared at the five sheets. It really did look bleak.

"Well," ventured Yasemin, "we wouldn't need in-house skills to build the website. We could partner with an experienced ecommerce firm."

"It wouldn't have to be Google, either," said David. "We could use a company like IBM to get artificial intelligence on the back end. Think Watson."

Michael said, "We could narrow our focus to eco-travel, or maybe bucket-list travel, so we'd have maximum credibility and efficiency. No need to boil the ocean to make a cup of tea."

The ideas were coming fast again. "We could have freemium pricing," said Talia. "Is that what they call it? Where the itineraries would be free, but customers would pay for premium services like personal travel agents."

"Good idea," said Michael with a smirk. "We could hire back some of the travel agents we'd be putting out of a job."

David suppressed a chuckle. He could always count on Michael to find the social angle.

"We could hire former travel agents for twenty-four seven helplines to take care of travelers with emergencies," said Talia. "Another premium service."

Michael read from his laptop: "It says here that travel agents make about $30,000 a year on average. We could afford to pay two or three times that much and build really strong bonds with premium customers."

Steve and Raven looked like spectators at a tennis match as Michael and Talia batted ideas back and forth over the net. David glowed. Here were his CFO and CMO, working together as if there were no daylight between finance and marketing.

Steve couldn't hold back. "If we went ahead and hired a bunch of ex-travel agents, we'd be right back where we started. In the goddamn people business. Isn't our payroll big enough already? Who wants more employees when the ones we've got are killing our profitability?"

"That's excellent black-hat thinking, Steve," said Shigeru, "but we're now on the green hat."

Steve crossed his arms and turned toward the blank wall.

Yasemin looked up from her laptop. "It says here, all things being equal, Internet eyeballs are worth eighteen times more than TV eyeballs. A large part of our revenues could come from advertising dollars."

David was dizzy with pride. Now his design chief was talking like a business strategist. What was the world coming to? He glanced at Gard.

Gard smiled back.

"Well, team, what do you think?" said David to the group at large. "Do we have the makings of a strategic coup?"

"I suppose we might," Raven admitted. "But we're missing even the most basic information to back up these assumptions."

"I agree," said Cary. "We're indulging in a lot of guesswork. Gard, what do you think?"

"Maybe. Could be. Might be. Two things stand out. First, nobody else seems to be doing it. That's a promising sign. Second, it would make a loopy kind of sense for BigSky to do it. Especially if we focused on eco-travel. At the same time, Steve is right. The company has fuck-all experience in the ecommerce space. Excuse my language."

"What's the next step?" said David.

"I think we should keep going and see how it pencils out. Meanwhile, Cary can vet our assumptions about customer needs. Let's spend the day tomorrow on a hypothetical brand position to see if it's ownable. Sound okay?" He glanced at David, then at the smiling faces around the room. There was near-unanimous support for his idea.

It was 6:00 p.m. Everyone was exhausted from the long day. But to David it seemed like no time at all, as if the hands had spun right off the clock.

ONLYNESS

Tuesday, December 21. David slathered cream cheese on both halves of a bagel and sat down at the dining table. Opening his laptop, he composed a quick note to Gard: *Late for this morning's session. Start without me.*

His meeting with the board was a little more than twenty-four hours away. He'd scheduled a 9:00 a.m. call with Andy to set expectations and gauge the mood of the board. If he failed to win them over tomorrow, the final presentation would be rough going. He hoped today's positioning workshop would spell the difference.

He scrolled through his contact list and tapped Andy's name. "Hi, Andy. Still a good time for you?"

"Of course. How've you been, David?

"Busy, as you can imagine. Things are going well. I'm pretty much set for tomorrow's check-in. I won't be bringing slides, but I can walk the board through our progress and lead a discussion." He remembered the meaning of *discutere*. A shiver rippled through his body.

"David, I have to tell you, the board is growing more skeptical by the day. The stock market's holding steady, but BigSky continues to tank. You probably saw this morning's flash report. We're losing ground."

"I know, Andy. We haven't been making our numbers, but I have some thoughts about that. By the end of the day I should have some key pieces of the puzzle in place. Don't expect a finished plan—just an informal here's-where-we-are, what-do-you-think? sort of presentation. We'll need the full five weeks to build everything out and test our assumptions."

"Okay, it's your show. I wanted you to know where we stood."

* * *

On his way in, David stopped by Brooks Brothers in Rockefeller Center to pick up the new suit he'd ordered. As his mother always said, "When the chips are down, dress up."

At 11:00 he slipped through the back door of the war room and took a seat. He knew if he recounted his conversation with Andy, he might spook the group and distort their work. Best to just keep everyone moving forward. He sat quietly and tried to absorb the latest output.

There were three large sheets on the wall, jammed with various positioning concepts. Colored dots clustered in different areas, apparently indicating which ideas had the most resonance. A fourth sheet, which seemed like a combined version of the first three, hung on the opposite wall.

"Morning, David!" said Shigeru, still wearing his blue Mets cap. "We forged ahead, as you requested. We just wrapped up the first exercise."

"Can you walk me through it?"

"Sure. Yesterday we nailed the third strategy question: where to compete. We think the website idea is solid. Today we're tackling the fourth Q about how we'll win. We've already agreed that the competition is not so much the other hotel chains as it is the general climate of uncertainty. Even so, we have to be mindful about where we'll end up when the climate improves and travel opens up. This morning Cary vetted our assumptions from yesterday. Cary, can you recap what you found?"

"I managed to schedule quick calls with seven potential customers over a range of travel types. I've got a dozen more scheduled for this afternoon."

"Nice work," David said admiringly.

"We aim to please. Of course, this is only preliminary, but I'm finding a common set of frustrations among travelers. Five out of seven said that travel was more difficult now than it was five years ago. Six said that travel agents no longer satisfied their desire for personalized trips. All seven said a website that produced detailed itineraries would be of moderate to great interest."

"Did you include any occasional travelers? People who think travel is out of reach?"

"Two of the people hadn't traveled since their pre-parenting days, mostly for cost reasons. They identified with the term *travel dreamers*. One said she would use the website as 'travel porn.'"

"Oh, great," said Steve. "Now we'll be arrested for indecency."

A few snickers.

"Our intention today is to zero in on the one thing that will make us unique in the marketplace," said Shigeru. "The goal is to avoid competition altogether, if possible, just as Andy did with the eco-lodges and airport hotels. To do this, we need to find our seminal *onlyness*."

David cocked his head. "Loneliness?" He certainly had the inside track on that one.

"*Only*ness," corrected Shigeru. "Being the only answer for the right set of customers, our chosen tribe. Being the number-one choice in our category."

"What *is* our category?"

"A fair question, which we discussed at length. Michael, do you want to tell David where we netted out?"

"Of course. First, we had to make a distinction between the BigSky brand and the new website brand. We're getting into territory where we have to think about brand architecture—how our various lines of business fit together in a larger house of brands. We can say that BigSky, the company, is the parent brand. Below that, the BigSky lodges, the Sojourner hotels, and the new website—whatever we end up calling it—are sub-brands." He drew the shape of a house on the board:

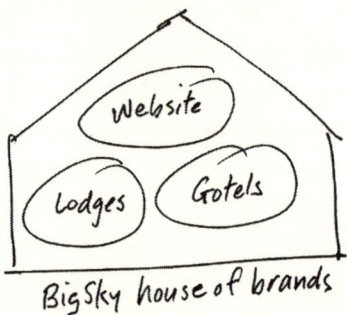

"All the sub-brands share the same DNA, the same core purpose of the parent brand: to democratize travel. But each sub-brand falls into a different category, with different competitors. Are you with me?"

"I think so," said David. "The nature hotels compete in the eco-lodge category. The Sojourners compete in the airport category. Seems straightforward enough. Where would the website compete?"

"We think the competitive set for the website, at least for now, would be online travel agencies. We'd probably be the first, or at least one of the first. There's no established category for online travel agencies, just a hodgepodge of travel information sites, online reservation companies, and brick-and-mortar agencies."

"And how would we position it?"

"That's what we're working on."

Cary stood up and walked over to the sheet containing the combined elements of the exercise. "We started by asking six general questions: *what* is our category, *how* do we compete, *who* are our customers, *where* do they live, *why* do they need us, and, finally, *when* do they need us. The idea is to lay out all the potential sources of onlyness to see which is the most powerful." She pointed to the answers on the sheet:

WHAT	The only online travel agency
HOW	that builds end-to-end itineraries
WHO	for those who long to visit distant lands
WHERE	all around the world
WHY	to complete their bucket lists
WHEN	in a time of increasingly difficult travel

Cary flicked an undisciplined strand of hair from her face. "Well, what do you think?"

"Sounds okay," David admitted. "We might change 'distant lands' to something more specific, like 'iconic nature destinations,' but maybe it's better to leave it open."

Steve spoke up. "The problem I have is not with the positioning of the business model, but the business model itself. Listen, if no other company is doing this, there's probably a good friggin' reason for it. Cary couldn't find one example of a company working in this category."

"Steve has a point," said Raven. "It's untried and extremely risky."

David looked around the room and saw pained looks on several faces. Apparently, he had missed one of Steve's outbursts. Before he could say anything, Gard broke in.

"If we want to capture a market position, we can't be followers. We have to lead. The trick here is to be narrow enough to own the category and broad enough to make money. I think we should suspend our doubts and keep pushing ahead. We'll still have time to try other strategies if we need to."

David silently disagreed. It was now or never. He'd already wasted the first two weeks with his dithering. They had to pull the whole strategy together in the remaining two weeks. His overriding concern was getting through tomorrow's meeting. Nothing else mattered.

"Onward and upward," he said, trying to sound confident. "Full speed ahead. The interim presentation is tomorrow. If the board doesn't buy into it, we'll deal with the consequences on Thursday."

Gard nodded. "It's 12:30 now. Let's break for lunch and get back to work in an hour."

David accompanied Gard to the cafeteria so he could hear what happened with Steve.

When the group returned from lunch, Shigeru put them to work in their teams. He asked them to look through their extended positioning statement and pull out the most compelling elements. The object was to edit the strongest ideas into a simple, clear expression of onlyness—no more than twelve words. As they headed to their separate working spaces, David asked Steve if they could have a few minutes alone. Steve followed him to the hallway.

"Steve," he said carefully, "I wonder if you realize your attitude is affecting the rest of the group."

"What do you mean?"

"You have to admit you can be a little negative."

Steve bristled. "Sorry, Davey boy, but that's the least of your problems right now. The money you're spending on Cultura would pay for a cost-reduction strategy from a top-of-the-line consulting firm. We're going off the rails here. Can't you see this whole website thing is crazy?"

"I do see that it's unusual. But we're in an unusual situation. I wonder if you could be a bit more upbeat for the sake of the group. You're a respected member of the team—people look to you for strength. I'm asking you to step up to the plate and be more positive. Do you think you can do that?"

Steve exhaled loudly. "Yeah, I can do that."

"Thanks. I appreciate it. We need you. BigSky needs you."

David began to see that he might require a few slides after all.

He mentioned this to Gard, who spoke with Cary. She agreed to work with David later in the afternoon to produce a clearly articulated slide deck—if the board's views were anything like Steve's, he would need as much help as he could get.

22

CHECKPOINT

Wednesday, December 22. David stood in BigSky's formal conference room with a remote in his hand. Notepads and water glasses formed perfect lines down each side of the long rosewood table. Soft lighting from custom-designed sconces reflected off mahogany-paneled walls, and a large flat-screen monitor faced him from the far end of the table. He clicked through his slides one more time before the board members arrived.

He and Cary had worked on the deck until 10:30 the night before. He'd told Andy the presentation would be informal, but now he was grateful for the added structure. He was also grateful to the salesperson at Brooks Brothers for fast-tracking his new suit. It felt like opening day at the ballpark, pitching the first game in a clean uniform. The chalk lines were painted on the field, the seats in the stands clean and shiny, and the grass green and freshly mown.

Andy was first to arrive. They shook hands, and Andy went down to the end of the table near the screen. He was all business. The others came in ones and twos. Within ten minutes the table was filled with a dozen board members. Andy stood and welcomed the group. He signaled David to begin.

"Thanks for coming, everyone. I know you have a million things on your plate with the holidays coming up. What I'd like to do is share the highlights of our progress toward a turnaround strategy. Given the seriousness of our situation, we've taken a bold approach, as you'll see. I'd like your feedback before we head into the final presentation on January 5."

The phrase "bold approach" got their attention. They'd all turned his way except for Phil Stine. Phil sat with a bored expression on his broad face, playing with a paperweight that he carried in this briefcase—a snow globe of the New York skyline. He turned it upside down and then right-side up, watching the snowflakes swirl in their orbit, like a giant contemplating his tiny kingdom.

Phil had been a highly successful hotelier for the last thirty years. He was tough, boorish, unimaginative, and famously unethical. How he got to be on BigSky's board was beyond David's comprehension. But he was certainly well connected.

David clicked to his first title slide: *The Problem.*

"We need to draw a distinction between our eco-lodge business and our airport business. As you know, the eco-lodges have suffered a serious drop in occupancy. This is impacting revenues and killing profitability, mostly because of fixed costs. Yet our average daily rate and customer satisfaction scores still lead the industry. The question is why—"

"David," interjected Barbara Henderson, a longtime board member. "Are you sure about the customer satisfaction scores? I just saw a one-star review of our lodge in Taos. The guest said the service had slipped, and she even found a dirty cleaning rag behind the toilet. What's going on?"

"I know about that, Barbara. It's true we've cut back on service in some of our lodges. Steve has spoken to the cleaner personally, and we think the incident is an outlier."

"You *think?*" said Andy, suddenly alarmed. "It takes a generation to build a reputation for quality. A few online reviews can destroy it."

Checkpoint

"Of course," said David, as calmly as he could. "The team and I agreed that cutting back on service is not the solution to our dilemma." He wasn't sure that Steve agreed, but he needed to get the presentation back on track. "The solution to our problem has got to address the underlying circumstances. As you can see, we're facing strong headwinds."

The next few slides laid out the causes of their predicament: a sudden slowdown in travel, a generalized mood of fearfulness, and airport security complications due to terrorist threats.

He then clicked to a slide titled *The Opportunity*. "If we can somehow take advantage of these circumstances, instead of simply enduring them, we think we can pull ahead of the competition and take full advantage of the eventual upturn." He emphasized that business as usual—even with substantially more effort and investment—would do nothing to change these forces. Instead, they had to get the headwinds to work in their favor.

His next slide, *A Radical Proposition*, went to the heart of the new strategy. It showed their proposed brand architecture, an outline of a house with three names in it: BigSky Lodges, Sojourner Inns, and Company X. Several of the members glanced at each other. *Company X*? Phil continued to play with his snow globe.

"The key insight came when we realized we were facing an *industry* problem instead of a *company* problem. The entire eco-travel category is suffering—not just BigSky. Those of you who run business hotels haven't experienced the same downturn. For example, our Sojourner chain is holding up pretty well. It's only the more remote eco-lodges that are underwater.

"Now," he said, changing to the next slide. "You're probably wondering about Company X. This is our bet. The idea is to build a third brand to take advantage of the headwinds I've just described." He heard murmurs as board members reacted to this news.

"Another business, David?" said Catherine, incredulous.

Catherine Hamilton was BigSky's largest shareholder after Phil—they sat on several important boards together. She'd inherited a "starter fortune" from her marriage to Roger L. Hamilton, who had founded a successful chain of business hotels. After he passed away, Catherine lost no time in proving she was much more than his arm-candy socialite wife. There were rumors of foul play surrounding her husband's death, but her legal and PR teams quickly quashed them. She took over the business and parlayed it into one of the biggest hotel empires in the US, with ambitions to expand internationally. She was tall, thin, and perfectly coifed, with diamonds the size of Alcatraz on several fingers.

"That's right," said David. "We plan to diversify. Our thought is to build the first online travel agency that offers free, end-to-end itineraries for bucket-list vacations. These are trips so important that people would face any number of fears, as long as they have control over the other variables."

"David, I don't understand. What is this, a website?"

"I think you could say it's a website on steroids, Catherine. There are plenty of travel websites, but none that use artificial intelligence to replicate the kind of personalized service that travel agents used to provide, but no longer can."

"Who else is doing this?" said Barbara.

"No one. That's the beauty of it. We'd be the first."

The murmurs grew louder. Phil hadn't looked up. He slowly turned the snow globe in his hands. Round and round it went, shrouding the city in a tiny blizzard.

"Imagine you're in the market for a trip. Let's say, Tibet. You know you want to go, but it's a big commitment and it's fairly complicated. You're not sure how to arrange all the pieces. Using our website, you could start by inputting your preferences. The AI engine would suggest a complete itinerary, free of charge, with every detail of the journey slotted in place. The complete time-

Checkpoint

line—flights, rental cars, hotels, excursions, restaurants, the whole works—scheduled down to the last detail. And if you wanted to change any details, no problem. You'd just click to see the alternatives, and there they'd be. You could tinker with your itinerary to your heart's content, all for free."

"Free?" said Catherine. "And how would we make money?"

"To be decided," said David. "We're working on it."

"And how would this new company help the eco-lodges?" said Barbara.

"Also TBD. At the very least there would be a knock-on effect from the website. But we won't be featuring our own lodges or airport hotels ahead of competitors. We think the credibility that comes with being agnostic will outweigh the negatives. We'll present every option according to its popularity with 'people like you.' We'll be Swiss in our approach to the travel wars."

"And where would this artificial intelligence come from?" said Catherine.

"Again, TBD. But we think we can rent it rather than building it ourselves."

The murmurs were swelling like a soft drumroll on a timpani. Suddenly there was a loud *bang* as Phil hammered his snow globe down on the table. He turned his large, scowling face toward David and inflated his body to its full height. His double-breasted suit made him look like an oversized chest of drawers.

"TBD, TBD. Everything is TBD and nothing makes any business sense. I've been listening to you, young man, and I don't think you know what the hell you're doing. This airy-fairy website of yours is pure fantasy. Why would you start a whole new business when you can't even fix the one we're in?"

David's mind raced. He wasn't prepared for such a hostile attack.

"One day," said Phil, "the lodges will be completely empty and you'll be telling us the good news is that the rates are holding up.

If you'd listened to the board in the first place and slashed prices, you wouldn't be in this predicament today." He lowered his body back into his chair and slowly shook his head. "I don't know, son. I'll have to defer to the chairman on this one."

Members on both sides of the table shifted their gaze from Phil to Andy. He looked distinctly uncomfortable.

"David, I have to side with Phil and Catherine. Your proposal seems half-baked. It's not at all what we expected, and it's missing too many critical pieces. Still, it's your company to run—at least for the next two weeks. I suggest you go back and fill in the blanks. Let's meet as planned on January 5."

The members rose and left the room as quickly as they'd come.

David was devastated. He felt as if his insides had been kicked out. He thought he'd made a reasonable case for diversifying the business. He didn't expect such a stinging rebuke. Even Andy had turned against him. He reached into his coat pocket. He pulled out his phone and typed a quick message: "I could use a lift."

The sky had acquired the color of a solar eclipse. Wispy curls of cirrus clouds shimmered dully in the spaces between buildings. The Prius was waiting at the curb. Sok's crooked smile faded to a frown as he read David's body language—slumped shoulders, stiff walk, sideways tie. He jumped out and opened the door.

"Wuzzah, stranger? You look like something the cat threw up."

David lowered himself into the back and dropped his bag on the seat beside him. "That sums it up perfectly," he said, leaning back and closing his eyes.

"Tell Mama."

"The board just ripped me a new one."

"Poor baby! What happened?"

David let out a long sigh. "As you know, we've been working on a new strategy. After three weeks of going round and round, I thought we'd finally nailed it. The board, however, disagreed. Now we've got two weeks left. We can either *a*, build a whole new strategy, or *b*, prove we were right in the first place. I tell you, Sok, I'm ready to go back to running an architecture firm. At least there I had something to show for a day's work."

Sokrates held up a hand. "Whoa, whoa. Slow down. First of all, how good was your strategy?"

"Amazing."

"Amazing. Meaning fresh, innovative, unique?"

"Yep."

"Okay, once upon a time, I was a car designer and you were an architect. So, tell me, how did you bring your clients along from the ordinary expectations they started with to a whole new vision?"

"What do you mean?"

"It's a simple question. How did you change their minds?"

"I never thought about it. I listened, talked, showed sketches, talked some more, made changes, did some pricing, built models, made some more changes. Then they signed off."

"Right. You worked with them in small steps. Me too. Now, in this case you've done all the work behind closed doors—at least from the board's point of view. Did you ever ask them what they were looking for?"

"No. Andy left it up to me."

"Okay, so you never asked what their expectations were, you kept them in the dark, and then you sprung a fully formed strategy on them. A bold one, I'm guessing. What did you expect?"

"I guess I expected them to be wowed."

"I'm sure they were, but not in a good way," he said, making a comical face in the mirror. "I'll bet if you'd given them something boring, like a reorg or an ad campaign, they would've bought it on the spot. Instead, you gave them…what?"

"An AI-driven—"

"Wait. Don't tell me. It's none of my business. You'll have to kill me afterward."

David failed to see the humor.

"Look, my man, you have the board at a disadvantage. You've been working on the problem solidly for three weeks. You've done the deep dive. As a designer, you have skills that most of them can't even imagine. Go slow. Tell them a story. Show some pictures. Bring them along step by step."

"What exactly is your advice?"

"Instead of starting over with a different strategy, come back with a better story. But, hey, you're the CEO. I'm just an Uber driver."

David shook his head. "I need a break, Sok. Take me home. We can talk in the morning."

"Sorry, man, didn't mean to pile on. Did I tell you the suit looks fantastic?"

David laughed against his will.

23

BLIZZARD

Thursday, December 23. The clouds had knitted a solid gray canopy over the city. David's mood, however, was a light-filled summer day. The time he'd spent alone in his apartment had brought his batteries back to full capacity.

The presentation to the board was certainly a setback, but at least it showed him what he was dealing with. A disruptive business on the scale he was proposing was bound to meet resistance. Where there's innovation, there's fear.

Go slow. Tell them a story. Show some pictures. Bring them along step by step. Like Sok said, the sticking point wasn't the strategy—it was the story. A much easier problem to fix.

Now he sat leaning forward in the back seat of the Prius, telling his new friend how much he appreciated him—his willing ear, his sense of humor, his sage advice. He wondered aloud how a kid from Queens had managed to accumulate such an impressive depth of wisdom.

"A wise man once said nothing," he replied.

"Seriously, you ought to charge for this."

"I will. You owe me $9.50 plus your usual crummy tip. Here we are at your building. Good luck with your team. Remember what you're going to tell them?"

"I think so. I'll say it went well for a first presentation, but we have work to do."

"Thattaboy. Now you're talking like a CEO."

"Jerk."

"Moron."

David punched Sokrates on the shoulder on his way out, then closed the door carefully with the tips of his fingers, as if it were the jeweled lid of a precious music box.

Their session was scheduled for 10:00, giving everyone time to catch up on their emails. When David entered the room, they were already there, waiting.

"Well?" said Talia. The cluster of fifteen faces looked like a nest of hungry birds, beaks open wide for their morning feeding.

He shook his head woefully for dramatic effect, then smiled and said, "Not too bad." The room erupted in cheers. He held up his hands. "Whoa, wait. We got approval to keep going with our concept, but some of the board members had concerns about how realistic our strategy was."

"Well, of course they did," said Michael. "We're just getting started."

"There's an old business saying," said Talia. "Never mistake a clear view for a short distance."

"Wise words," said David. "Gard, what if we spend the day learning more about the travel agency business, the best practices of e-commerce, the latest techniques in web design, and everything we can about the competition?"

"Sounds good to me."

"Can you and your team hang out here and help us gather information?"

"Sure, we're booked at BigSky today and tomorrow. We're breaking for Christmas Day, right?"

"That's the plan—proving Ebenezer Stone has a heart after all."

Talia stifled a laugh.

"Let's meet back here at 3:00 and see where we stand."

In the afternoon, they reconvened with their arms full of laptops, magazines, printouts, and large sheets with sticky notes plastered on them.

"We can load our findings onto the intranet," said David. "But for now, let's just go around the room so each of us can share one interesting tidbit with the group. Talia, want to start?"

She stood up. "I learned that travel agencies are mostly selling cruise vacations these days, with secondary revenues coming from tours and package deals. The number of airline tickets sold by travel agents, according to the ASTA website, has shrunk to 50 percent. But that number is ten years old, and ASTA has been slow to update it. The latest figures show that airline tickets are actually more like 20 percent of the business and dropping."

"What does that tell us?"

"That the travel agency business sucks," said Steve. "And we should run like hell."

David ignored him. "Anyone else?"

"To me, it says traditional agencies can't compete with online alternatives," said Michael. "They can't offer the same level of comparative shopping or convenience."

Gard turned his laptop around to face the group. "Here's how travel agents defend their roles against online competitors." He enlarged the text on the screen:

> *While the Internet is a valuable resource, it can't replace the expertise, guidance, and personal service of a travel agent.*

"Expertise, guidance, and personal service. Sounds like wishful thinking to me. As soon as websites can offer these at a lower price, the entire industry will move online."

"In related news," said David, "I found that travelers, on average, visit twenty-six websites to plan a single vacation. *Twenty-six!* And more than half of these travelers do their research on smartphones, the total of which has doubled to 2.5 billion over the last five years. If we could shrink those twenty-six websites down to one, my guess is that people might buy $10,000 packages from their phones."

"Especially if we add some compelling social elements," said Yasemin, "like forums where people can easily socialize and share their experiences. They'd need to be open and welcoming, of course, so noncustomers could interact with customers and expand the tribe."

"Would Cultura agree with that?" said David.

"Absolutely," replied Cary. "Ten years ago, less than 10 percent of people contributed online content. Now it's up to 80 percent. People are finding a lot of value in these forums."

Gard spoke up. "Cary, have you gathered any more insights from travelers?"

"I spent all day yesterday with potential customers. Most of what they said reinforced my first seven calls. But this time I went more granular with my questions. I got a sense of how, where, when, and with whom people decide to explore a vacation."

The group listened attentively.

"The answer's complicated," she said, "but a few things stand out. Most people want to travel not just to visit relatives or take their kids to Disney World. They harbor dreams of magical vacations to special destinations. Trips to beautiful nature resorts like ours, but also cities like the big three in Europe: Paris, Rome, London.

"More surprising, though, is *why* they want to travel. They believe travel will complete them in some way. Even if it's a single blowout vacation to Florence or Kyoto, some people plan for it their whole lives. A few said their biggest regret was putting off a trip to their family's home country. We joke about bucket-list travel, but people feel diminished when they can't realize a long-cherished dream."

The team members grew quiet as they absorbed the poignancy of Cary's findings. She went on to describe the details of how people made their decisions, paid for their trips, and spent their precious few weeks of travel.

"Speaking of people's lives," said Michael. "It says here that more than two-thirds of consumers want online companies to play a stronger role in improving their lives. Only one quarter believe that companies are actually doing it."

"That may be true," said Raven. "But if one company offers customers more goodies than another company, it won't be long before other companies follow, if only in self-defense. It's like a gas war. The companies would end up competing away their profits."

"Interesting point, Raven," said David, pleased she was finally joining in. "You could imagine a 'love war,' as one company tried to out-please the other."

"Or the opposite," said Michael. "A disruptive company could face vicious, even underhanded attacks from traditional companies who felt threatened."

"How can we avoid that?" said David.

"One solution might be to give competitors a role," said Raven. "The researchers at Forester say companies should re-envision themselves as part of an ecosystem instead of standalone companies. They should let customers assemble the relevant pieces according to their needs."

"Once again, that argues for agnosticism," said Michael. "If we ever started favoring our own properties over those of competitors, we'd damage the spirit of coopetition."

"The spirit of what?" said Talia, eyebrows raised over her glasses.

"*Coopetition*: competitors who cooperate for mutual benefit."

"What would Shakespeare say about that?"

"Keep your friends close, and your enemies closer."

"No way!" she said. "That was Michael Corleone in *The Godfather*!"

Michael faked a guilty expression. "Busted."

David walked to the front of the room. "All right, everyone," he said. "We're down to our final two weeks. Let's give a big hand to all our GMs and VPs who took time out of their busy schedules to pitch in." The group complied with a heartfelt burst of applause. "Our strategic direction is pretty much set, so you seven can go back to your normal duties. The rest of you, please stay."

There were hugs and well-wishes as the excused team members gathered up their things to leave.

"Now that we're down to a smaller group," David said, "we'll need to shift into high gear. How many people can stay late tonight?"

Eight hands went up—the entire core team: Talia, Michael, Yasemin, Steve, Raven, and the three people from Cultura.

"Great. I'll be joining you. There's only one hitch. As you've probably heard, the weather is calling for a snowstorm, which could hit in the next two hours or so. It may not materialize, but there's a chance we could be snowed in. Anyone whose work is not essential should leave now and work from home."

The eight members glanced at one another. No one made a move. They couldn't bear the thought of their contributions as "not essential," especially with the future of the company at stake—and only two weeks until "D-day."

"You guys are champs," said David. "I can't tell you how much I appreciate your energy and support, especially with Christmas coming up."

By 5:30 a cold wind was whipping litter into small eddies under the streetlights. At 6:00 the first few flurries appeared, dancing with abandon outside the windows. David had asked the cafeteria to send up a stack of pizzas before shutting down for the night. The group hardly noticed the snowflakes as they thickened into tufts, then formed into horizontal streaks driving fiercely toward the southwest.

24

CHRISTMAS EVE

Friday, December 24. If anything, the blizzard had intensified. The Weather Channel had reclassified it a Category 4 "nor'easter," a dangerous storm calling for the utmost caution. There were reports of power outages, accidents, property damage, and even deaths. The subway had shut down completely, as had the airports. Amtrak reported closures due to frozen track switches. The only taxicabs were those abandoned in the streets—large, shapeless lumps of icy cotton. A feud between the city and the sanitation union accounted for the absence of snowplows. Seven o'clock in the morning found the bedraggled team in various stages of waking. Some had slept under desks, others had found couches in other parts of the building. David had skipped sleep altogether and worked through the night. So had Michael.

David made two capuccinos with the new Gaggia espresso machine he'd insisted on buying for the breakroom—he was now grateful for his foresight. He and Michael stood before the window, drinks in hand, watching the wind draw a continuous curtain of white slurry across the view.

"Bloody blizzard," said Michael.

"Unbelievable," said David.

"Who do you have to kill for a cup of tea around here?" said a voice from behind.

They turned. It was Cary, hands on hips, hair sticking out in every direction. David couldn't suppress a laugh.

"Go ahead, make fun," she said. "But if someone doesn't get me a cup of tea in about ten seconds, I can't be responsible for what happens next." David apologized and rushed off to the breakroom. "With milk!" she yelled after him.

Michael asked how she slept.

"I think my hair tells the story."

"So it does. Complete with plot twists and a surprise ending."

"That's enough outta you, Brit Boy."

David came back with a cup and saucer cradled in his hands.

"My hair thanks you. I'll be fine after this."

Before long the group was back in the war room, if somewhat worse for wear. No workers could get into the city, including BigSky's kitchen staff. Gard had scrounged a tray of day-old donuts, bagels, and croissants from the cafeteria. The team fell upon these as if a prisoner's last meal. David's eyelids felt like sandpaper. He secretly longed for a bath.

"Good morning?" he said with a question mark. He was greeted with a mixture of jeers and good-natured grousing.

"As you can see," he said, "the weather shows no sign of letting up. With any luck, we'll get a break this afternoon. You'll be able to go home for Christmas and be with your family. Or, if you're like me, your king-size mattress. In the meantime, let's continue to explore the terrain of our new brand. I'll see what we can do about getting some lunch up here. Maybe by then we'll know more about the weather situation. We have the whole building to ourselves, so work anywhere you like."

As they set off for parts unknown, David ducked into his office and called his parents. It was Christmas Eve, and he still felt guilty about canceling his holiday visit.

His mother answered, and he knew immediately something was wrong. She'd been crying.

"Mom, what's the matter?"

"Your father's in the hospital. I just got back a few minutes ago."

"What?"

"He had a stroke last night. I phoned *911*. I feel terrible about it. He always told me, 'Never call an ambulance—they cost too much.' But what could I do?"

"Mom, what *happened?*"

"He collapsed in the bathroom last night before bedtime. The doctor said he'd had a mild stroke on the left side of his brain. He was unconscious at the hospital all night, and when he woke up he couldn't speak."

David's mind was reeling. He knew he had to be there, but travel was out of the question. "Mom, I'm trapped in a blizzard. Hold tight. I'll be there as soon as I can."

"No, David, please don't. There's nothing you can do. The doctor says he'll probably make a good recovery, and right now your company needs you. Dad would want you to keep working. I'm sure he'd rather see you when he's back on his feet."

"When will that be?"

"I don't know. Maybe a few days? Maybe a week? I'll stay over-

Christmas Eve

night at the hospital. I just came home to pack a few things."

David was beside himself. Suddenly the job, the company, his 3,500 employees—none of it meant anything.

"Mom, I need to be there with you and Dad."

"You will. Just give it a few days and we'll see how he does."

David hung up and slumped in his chair. If his mother says he'll be all right, he'll be all right. On the other hand, stoicism is part and parcel of farm life. What if she's just putting a good face on it? Either way, he felt helpless. He resolved to keep the news to himself—there was no benefit in distracting the rest of the team.

At four o'clock that afternoon, he called everyone into the war room. The storm had taken a seat over the entire region and showed no signs of getting up. "You'd better call your families. Tell them you love them," he said wistfully, "but you won't be home for Christmas. We're here for the duration."

The group emitted a collective groan.

"All I can say is," said Michael, "we're lucky we have a lot of space here. You won't want to be around me after one more night."

"I don't want to be around you right now," said Steve.

Talia jabbed him in the ribs.

"I have an idea," said David. "We can't get out of the city, but we *can* get across the street. Let's head over and take rooms at the hotel. We can get cleaned up and meet for dinner in the restaurant. In the morning, we'll come back and keep working if the storm hasn't moved on."

They looked at each other in horror.

"In the Bull Building?" said Yasemin. "Shoot me now."

The others expressed similar feelings. Yet the prospect of a hot shower and real food was too much to resist. They reluctantly agreed to go and bundled up for the trek through the bleak and blinding whiteness of the storm.

* * *

The registration desk was eerily deserted. A soundtrack of Christmas carols played blandly for no one in particular. They waited on the pink and black marble floor of the lobby for a receptionist.

"Wow," said Yasemin, under her breath. "Look at all this gold."

Michael leaned toward her, close enough to whisper in a low voice, "All that glitters is not gold. This just proves bad taste is hard to hide."

Yasemin involuntarily pulled back—Michael's odor was exactly as advertised. The receptionist finally came out, straightening her jacket. They took their keycards and went to their respective rooms, desperate for showers and laundry service.

At 7:30 they met for dinner at the Bullpen, a spacious steak restaurant in the top-floor atrium. A few couples were scattered here and there, along with a table of business people, four men dressed uniformly in dark suits, no ties.

The same Christmas soundtrack as in the lobby emanated from the tops of artificial palm trees, their plastic trunks wrapped in spiral strings of white lights. The waiter passed around oversized gold-lamé menus with gold tassels.

"Look at this," said Raven, her finger on one of the choices. "A hundred-dollar, seventy-two-ounce steak. Do you think anyone would actually order that?"

"I would," said Steve. "I'm starving."

David shared the sentiment. The food they'd scrounged from the cafeteria was less than inspiring. They placed their orders and helped themselves to Parmesan-flavored breadsticks. The waiter brought back a bottle of Sea Smoke pinot noir and appetizers for the table. Michael peered into his phone.

"Technology is amazing," he said. "It enables so many wonders.

Among these, apparently, is the elevation of ignorance."

"What are you talking about?" said Cary. Her hair was under new management—a red barrette securing the insubordinate spray.

"It's one thing to send a never-ending series of crackpot tweets, but it's another thing to misspell them. Here's the latest from the proprietor of this fine establishment." He turned his phone for the others to see:

> *Were keeping America #terror-free fro the hollidays. Merry chrismas!*

"Ouch," said Cary. "Editorial emergency. But I do feel safer now."

"Let's hope Santa can get through security," said Talia.

Yasemin had been staring at the ceiling. "That's a lot of glass," she said. They all raised their eyes. "I bet this room is beautiful on a sunny day. I mean, if you could take out the fake palm trees and gold chandeliers."

"Architecturally, it's a nice space," said David. "The big failing for me is the complete lack of sustainability."

"Their heating and cooling costs must be through the roof," Steve said, chortling at his little joke.

Yasemin stared. "Seriously, if we could figure out how to solve the energy problem, we could build ceilings like this in some of our lodges."

"Mm," said Michael, looking up. "Imagine a glass ceiling in the high Chilean desert, where the stars are thick as spilled sugar. The chairs in the restaurant could recline, and after dinner we could turn out the lights and serve pisco sours under the glow of the southern sky."

They took a few seconds to imagine this scene.

"That reminds me," said Yasemin. "I met a Chilean architect at a sustainability conference last spring. He used solar glass on the western and southern exposures of a skyscraper in Santiago. The solar collectors are transparent, so you get net-zero energy usage with maximum light pass-through. We could build huge atriums like this that actually conserve energy."

"Nice idea," said Gard. "At least Bull's been good for something tonight."

"Don't be so hard on him," said David. "As my grandfather used to say, 'Never criticize a man until you've walked a mile in his shoes. That way you'll be a mile away, and you'll have his shoes.'"

It may have been the exhaustion. It may have been the red wine. But they laughed so hard that the four businessmen stopped talking and swiveled around to look. Raven leaned forward and whispered, "Do you think those guys are off-duty secret service?" This produced further howls.

David stood up and raised his glass. "To the strangest Christmas ever." They clinked glasses. "Happy holidays."

"With two *L*s," said Cary.

David laughed along with the others, but all he could think about was his father in the hospital, and his mother coping alone.

25

GIFTS

Saturday, December 25. They had agreed to meet in a lower-level restaurant for breakfast on Christmas morning.

The hotel had run out of fresh produce, so the cooking staff had repurposed its leftover ingredients into fish omelets, breakfast tacos, and steak-and-potato quiche. This was standard operating procedure on Sundays and Mondays when suppliers were closed—

Gifts

all the staff had to do was move it forward a day. The waiter apologized; David smiled and said they were happy to have it.

By 8:45 the snowplows had come through and the blizzard had abated somewhat. The snow was still falling, but the wind had changed to intermittent gusts. The Weather Channel was predicting a chance of clear skies by the evening. The city's transportation was still not operational—a few trains were running, but the subways hadn't reopened and there were no taxis or cars to be seen.

David and the team donned their heavy coats and headed across the street. He glanced up at the Bull logo on top of the building. It was mounded high with fresh drifts of snow. Not exactly the white Christmas they were hoping for, but nothing about this holiday had been traditional.

Shigeru, always the planner, had ordered a to-go box of stuffed potatoes—half with Brie and ham, and the other half with veggies and goat cheese. They could heat these in the microwave if they were still stuck in the office at lunchtime.

David asked them to put in one more morning of work. Afterward they could relax, he said, and with any luck return to their homes in the evening.

He called his mother to wish her a merry Christmas. She had good news. His father was awake and cooperating with the hospital therapist to bring back his speech and his ability to swallow. She said he was already talking a little, but mixing up his words. David promised to check back tomorrow and told her how much he loved them both.

Gard had suggested that the team make use of the Christmas spirit to imagine "gifts" BigSky could offer its customers—special experiences or benefits that came from a place of goodwill instead of profit-making. This struck everyone as a fine idea. They filed into the conference room at 10:30, bringing cups of coffee and tea.

At each seat, they found a tiny wrapped present—a one-inch

blue box topped with a flower, a folded rosette made of yellow paper. Inside each box was a cocoa-dusted chocolate truffle.

"Who did this?" said Raven. She looked at David. He nodded toward Talia.

"I just wanted to show you all how much I appreciate you," she said. "This is the best team I've ever been on. If nothing else works out—if the board rejects our strategy, if we all lose our jobs—I'll always treasure this time together." She stifled a small sob, then laughed with embarrassment. "The team across the street is probably getting cocoa-dusted coal." Yasemin put her arm around Talia and kissed her cheek.

"Tally, where did you get these?" said Michael.

"They were a gift from a supplier. I was saving them for a special occasion." She reached for Yasemin's hand. "Yaz helped me make the boxes out of old file folders and the flowers out of sticky notes."

They suddenly saw Talia in a different light. She'd always been the pragmatic, sensible one. But now they beheld the loving, even sentimental one. David was grateful for her steadying influence, and at that moment realized she was probably the unofficial mom of the company.

"How did you make the flowers?" said Michael.

"Show 'em, Yaz."

Yaz peeled off a yellow sticky note and hid it in her left hand. She smoothed her right hand over her left, opening both hands in the shape of a cup. Cradled inside was a perfectly formed paper flower. They gasped.

"Let me guess," said Michael. "Child's play."

Yasemin looked at him as if he were an interesting zoo specimen. "No, origami."

They laughed and began sharing their ideas for customer gifts. There were the usual freebies, bonuses, specials, and acknowledgments. When it was Raven's turn, however, she took the exercise

Gifts

in a new direction.

"I reversed the assumptions," she said, "using the pinballing technique we learned. I thought, What are the common beliefs about companies who move their businesses online? How could we reverse them?

"One belief," she continued, "is that when customers have a problem with a service, or a company, or its website, the responsibility for solving it is theirs. They have to call up, work their way through a series of voice-recognition gates, line up their facts, make a clear case, and then be shuttled from one so-called specialist to another until the problem is solved. In some cases, they'll get a message telling them to try again during business hours." Everyone nodded, recalling such frustrating experiences.

"A related belief is that call centers must be manned by either low-salaried employees or outsourcing companies with even lower-salaried employees." She paused to make sure the group was following.

"So?" said Steve.

"So," she said, "what if we did the opposite?"

"What do you mean 'the opposite'?" said David.

"I mean, what if we staffed our call center with highly paid experts?"

Steve shook his head in disbelief. "I think you've mixed up your meds, Raven. You're talking about a huge investment in labor."

"Maybe. But think about it: companies use call centers to make up for glitches in the system. If the system were designed better, the number of calls would be lower, and so would the costs. If we had inquisitive, thoughtful people taking these calls, we'd know which glitches needed to be fixed. We could fix them faster and lower our labor costs."

"Aha," said Yasemin. "The number of calls would act as a metric. More calls would signal poor design. Fewer calls would signal better design. The challenge would be to bring the number of calls closer to zero by bringing the design up to a hundred."

"Exactly. In the meantime," Raven continued, "every problem exposed by a customer would be another chance to create a deeper level of trust. One thing I've learned as head of revenues is that there's no stronger bond than the bond you create from acknowledging—and fixing—a problem that you yourself caused."

"Great insight," said David.

"That could be our gift, both to them and to us," she said. "I'd put the smartest, most empathetic people I could find on the front lines." Her counterintuitive idea seems to take everyone by surprise. It seemed so wrong it was right.

David was about to say something when they heard a tortured squeal, like fingernails on a giant blackboard, outside the window. Through the swirling snowflakes, across the street, they saw a giant letter *B* tearing loose from the weight of the snow. It twisted and turned against the glass of the Bull building's façade, then broke free and dropped to the street below. They ran to the window and saw the gold-painted *B* crumpled in a heap on the snow-covered sidewalk. Luckily, no one was injured. The signage on the building now said ULL.

Their jaws fell open. They looked blankly at each other. No one spoke.

Finally, Michael said, "What we have here is a logo with an existential crisis."

"To *B* or not to *B*," added Cary.

"Hey, that was my line!" said Michael.

Instantly, their horror turned to hilarity, and the puns began to fly.

"As Shakespeare would say, '*B gone!*'"

"Talk about killer *B*s," said Steve.

"It's the ULL-timate revenge," said Talia.

* * *

Gifts

At the end of the session, David offered his compliments on a good morning's work. He sent them to the breakroom to heat up the stuffed potatoes that Shigeru had bought for lunch. They spent the afternoon chatting, making calls to family members, and playing online Scrabble. Michael was winning, not surprisingly. Talia said it wasn't fair to compete against someone who does the London *Times* crossword puzzle in ink. When he placed the letters *U, L,* and another *L* on the board, he sent the group into hysterics.

At 4:30 David confirmed with the city transportation department that the streets had been cleared and the subway was back in operation. He'd just gotten off the phone when he heard a commotion in the war room. He ran over and stuck his head around the corner. Steve had been arguing with Gard and Michael about Raven's idea.

"All these do-gooder schemes are bullshit," he said, his voice gaining volume. "No one can devote expensive resources to call centers. It's absurd. There's a reason why companies outsource their customer service. It's cheaper! I'm sick of all this pie-in-the-sky brainstorming crap. We need to get real here." Michael was about to object when he saw David walk in.

"Hey, guys," said David in his best fatherly voice. "It's Christmas." He put his hand on Steve's shoulder. "Let's try to be a little more supportive. Raven was doing her best to be helpful."

They heard a small noise at the back of the room. They turned and saw Raven silhouetted in the doorway. She froze for a second, then spun away and was gone. David clenched his eyelids.

He quickly gathered the team in the war room. Sitting on the edge of a table, he thanked them for their perseverance, their professionalism, and especially their willingness to work through the holidays. "I know you're all extremely tired. I just wanted to say how proud you've made me. You're good soldiers, all of you." He looked into each of their faces. Talia was close to tears. Yasemin looked at Raven with newfound admiration. Michael and Shigeru exchanged victorious smiles. Gard took a deep breath, and Cary leaned her head on his shoulder. Steve stared at the wall.

"I just called the city. The streets are being cleared and the subway is running. Let's take tomorrow off and try to salvage what's left of our weekend. Meet me back here on Monday, bright and early. All right?"

Everyone but Steve exchanged warm hugs and holiday wishes, laughing and chatting as they took the lifts down to the lobby in small groups. The last face David saw was that of his COO, glowering darkly as the elevator doors closed in front of him.

26

ANXIETY

Sunday, December 26. Back in his apartment, David felt free. No distractions, no lingering holiday obligations, and no Christmas cards to open—the storm had halted all mail delivery. He'd call his mother in the afternoon to allow for the three-hour time difference.

The freedom he felt was tempered by the knowledge of his pending deadline. He knew Andy would be of little help, and might even be actively working against him. They say there comes a moment in every mentorship when the protégé grows strong enough to act independently. The mentor can feel betrayed and even denounce the protégé. A wave of sadness swept through David, followed by a wave of something else—exhilaration? Deep tides were shifting.

He pulled a notebook from the shelf and settled into the Eames lounge chair he'd bought as a young architect. He had to admit

Anxiety

that its cradle-like leather-and-plywood forms were not as comfortable as the mythology would have it. The iconic chair served more as a talisman than a functional piece of furniture. It was probably time to leave such obvious symbols behind. He now had his own design principles, including a few that he'd recently learned through working with the strategy team.

Where were they now? They'd been struggling with the strategy for twenty days. It seemed like a lifetime. In the beginning the team was nowhere, groping through the darkness in a random search for answers. There was very little cohesion. David had managed to develop some trust among the members, but their ideas still lacked focus.

Then, with Gard's help, they started to get traction. They worked their way through three of the five Qs, starting with the company's purpose and ending with David's idea to launch a first-of-its-kind website. On the way, they learned how to use the five Ps of design thinking: problemizing, pinballing, probing, prototyping, and proofing. These formed the essence of *agile strategy*, the term Cultura used to describe this new, accelerated approach to planning.

Opening the notebook to a blank page, he wrote at the top: *What have we learned?* He began making a list.

First, they'd learned that real progress was impossible without a strong sense of shared purpose. Beyond that, every company needed a way to stand out from the competition—a compelling point of difference. Onlyness, as Cultura called it. But they couldn't develop their onlyness until they truly understood their customer tribe.

They'd learned that a brand was essentially a reputation, not a logo or a product. As such, it's not built by the company, but by customers. It's what *they* say it is, not what *the company* says it is. The company creates the customers; the customers build the brand.

He turned to the next blank page and wrote: *What have I*

learned? He'd learned, courtesy of Sokrates, that trust starts at the top. It wasn't until he'd started to trust his staff that they opened up to him. He'd also learned that leaders, by definition, needed empowered followers. CEOs who try to do everything themselves aren't leaders but one-man bands.

Okay, what else? He'd learned it's not a sign of weakness to hire experts. There was no way he and his staff could duplicate the broad experience and independent thinking of a firm like Cultura. Their system for building a strategy was brilliant—simple, powerful, and exceedingly fast. Of course, David's training as an architect didn't hurt. He imagined that leaders without creative experience might chafe against all the unknowns.

Finally, he'd learned that coming up with a breakthrough idea did not guarantee the board's support. He and the strategy team would need a compelling story, one calculated to bring the outsiders on a journey from their initial preconceptions to an elevated view of the possibilities. This was the next task they would face.

He closed the notebook and gazed out the window. The sky was clear in the wake of the storm. A welcome blast of sunshine threw geometric patterns across the blonde hardwood floor. He thought about his father and reached for the phone.

"David!" his mother answered brightly. "Your dad's here."

"How is he?"

"He's awake, he's happy, and doing well with his therapy sessions. He's swallowing a little better, but his speech has a way to go."

"Can I talk to him?"

"Yes! He's been asking for you."

"Hi, Dad," said David. "I've been so worried. I'm going to fly out to see you as soon as I can."

"No. D-d…don't come. Fine." His words seem be getting lost somewhere between his brain and the phone. "You keep…water… no, work…"

His mother grabbed the phone. "He understands everything you're saying, but he can't articulate his thoughts. Wait—he wants to talk again."

"Dav…remember the bat…barn…we made?"

"Of course I do, Dad."

"Still…it still…" All David could hear were guttural sounds as his father struggled to form his words.

His mother came back on the phone. "What he wants to say is that the barn you two built is still working exactly the way you designed it. He's so proud of you. He thinks—wait. Here he is again."

"You…so good at see…see new path…new pass…" His voice was raspy and rough. David could hear his mother taking the phone back.

"He told me you're so good at seeing new possibilities because you work from—what did he say?—first principles. He's nodding. First principles. And you should have faith in your abilities."

David had to fight back the tears when his father came on again.

"Da…fid. Don't…don't you gif *up*." It seemed to take all his energy to complete the sentence.

"Dad, I love you. I miss you so much. I wish I were with you, building the barn all over again. I was never so happy as I was then."

"Don't gif *up*!" he said in a gruff and gravelly voice, dropping the phone.

"David, are you still there? Don't worry. He sounds worse than he is. You should have heard him yesterday, nothing but grunts and groans. He wants you to wait until after your big presentation before you visit us. Remember what he used to say? 'Come back with your shield or on it.'"

"That's Dad," said David with a sniffling laugh. "I'm so glad he's doing better. Talk to you soon, Mom. Love you."

His father had sounded awful. But at the same time, there was something profound in his effortful encouragement, like an exhausted runner handing the baton to a fresh one. It was as if he didn't want his own accomplishments to end with the inevitability of death. David would be his emissary into the future.

He went to the kitchen and poured a glass of water. Normally, on a Sunday afternoon, it wouldn't be water but a cold Riesling or Sauvignon blanc. But now he was in training. He resolved to come back *with* his shield.

He thought about Sokrates. Here was someone who would never feel the firm hand of a loving father on his back, guiding him forward, lending him strength. David was acutely aware that so many of his recent personal insights had come from Sokrates. How did he get so wise without a father to teach him?

There was something tugging at the edge of David's consciousness, a nagging anxiety that refused to come into focus. What was it? He sat down and set the water on the side table. There was something holding the team back—not completely, but enough to slow them down. They'd been working well together, despite the stress of the blizzard and missing their holidays. They were clicking. Ideas were flowing, their confidence gaining day by day. Even Raven had surprised him, coming up with the richest insight of the day.

Raven, he thought. Bird. Hummingbird. That was it.

They had a hummingbird in the house, drawing attention away from their work. When he thought back over the last few weeks, he realized that Steve hadn't contributed a single useful idea. Worse, he seemed to be sapping everyone else's strength. Why hadn't he seen it before? David would have to act, and soon. They were down to ten days.

27

JONAH

Monday, December 27. He badly needed a sounding board. Andy had all but deserted him, and he couldn't involve Gard in internecine issues. After putting away the breakfast dishes, he texted Sokrates.

Yesterday's blue skies had given way to the darkening clouds of another low-pressure system. The sidewalks were packed with shoppers returning gifts and picking up post-Christmas bargains. To David, it was a parallel universe. All he could think about was his mission to save the company. How was it possible that other people could be so relaxed and carefree?

As Sokrates drove them up Tenth Avenue, David explained the situation with Steve—how he discouraged the team by discounting the contributions of the members, even disparaging the mission itself.

"Who is he?"

"The COO. Everyone had assumed he was next in line for CEO, but I was chosen instead. He works hard, gets things down, never misses a day's work."

"He sounds like a paragon," said Sokrates.

"He's the driving engine of the company."

"What's the problem?"

"He's also abrasive, misogynistic, and vaguely racist. He revels in playing devil's advocate. He thinks employees are naturally lazy and tends to rule by intimidation. Some of these traits have leaked into our strategy sessions. A few of the members have complained about his defeatist attitude."

"Is he doing the work?"

"He comes to the meetings," said David, "but he's not really there. You might say he's present but absent. I realized yesterday that he hasn't contributed one solid idea the whole time we've been working together. When he's not shooting down other people's ideas, he sits there with nothing to say."

"So he's good with daily routines, but in a creative setting, with fewer guideposts, he's lost. His modus doesn't operandi."

"You could say that," said David.

Sokrates slowed the car, then pulled over to the curb. He turned and looked David in the eye.

"I think you've got a Jonah."

"What?"

"A Jonah. From the Bible. Jonah takes passage on a sailing ship. A hurricane comes up and threatens the lives of everyone on board. In desperation, they start praying to their various gods. They notice that Jonah isn't praying with them. He's down in the hold, sleeping. You don't know this story?"

"No. What happens?"

"They start throwing stuff overboard. They dump everything they can find, including the cargo. Nothing works. They start to believe Jonah is bad luck, and the only way to save the ship is to throw *him* overboard. Which they do. Immediately, the storm quiets down and they head safely toward shore."

"Are you saying Steve has to go overboard?"

"Not my call. You're the captain."

David gazed dolefully out the window, the grayness of the morning enveloping everything—the sky, the buildings, his thoughts, his hopes for the future.

He closed the door to his office. He threw his bag on the sofa and sat down next to it. He knew Sokrates was right. The best thing to do, both for Steve and the company, was to remove him from the

Jonah

strategy team and return him to operations.

He called Gard, who was relieved to hear the news. He too had been feeling the drag on their progress. They agreed to resume the strategy work tomorrow, giving David some time to deal with Steve and allowing the others to check in with their respective departments. Every day they spent working on strategy was another day their assistants had to cover for them. He sent a group email with the revised schedule. He sent a second email to Steve, asking for a meeting.

At 4:00 Steve knocked on David's door. His face showed the same frown he'd been wearing the other day. He seemed to sense what was coming.

"Hi, Steve. Thanks for being on time. Please sit down."

"I prefer to stand."

"Suit yourself. I'll get to the point. I'm taking you off the strategy project. I'd like you to go back to your regular duties, starting tomorrow."

His tendons stiffened. "Why?"

"I don't think the work suits you. And, to be honest, your attitude has been affecting the rest of the team."

"My *at-ti-tude*." He spit out the syllables as if they were coated with castor oil.

"We talked about this before. I've asked you—more than once—to be supportive of the other team members. You apparently found it difficult. More to the point, you haven't contributed any ideas yourself."

"Why, because I couldn't think of any stupid carnets or starry, starry nights for our imaginary guests in Chile? This whole exercise has been a waste of resources."

David took a breath. "It hasn't, Steve. We've made great strides, and I think we're well on the way to a yes decision from the board."

Steve's lips contorted into a snarl. "You've taken this company and driven it into the ground. You want me to run back to my little office while you turn BigSky into a fucking Internet company. Sorry, pal, I'm not on board. I'd rather work for a company that knows what it's doing than a shit parade that chases every last fad off a cliff. There's no way I'm leaving the strategy to you and your Little League friend. You'll have to fire me." Steve's chin was two inches from David's. He stared defiantly, waiting for a response.

David sighed. "Steve, you're not fired. You're too important to the company. I truly appreciate how you keep us on track. It's what you're good at. What I'm saying is that you're not quite as good with the strategy stuff."

"Oh, really?" he said, eyes red with blood. "Strategize *this*." He shoved a middle finger in David's face.

"That's it," said David. "Box up your crap and get the hell out of here. Leave your computer and all your files. I'll have HR square everything in the morning."

Steve jabbed his finger at David twice. "Fuck. You." He turned on his heel and stormed down the hallway to his office. David could hear drawers slamming, books hitting the floor. He quietly closed his door and sat on the sofa. Now what?

He finally sent an email to the team: *Meet me in the war room.*

When they were all seated, he dropped the bomb. "I just dismissed Steve. He'll be locked out of the building in the morning."

Stunned silence.

"I wanted you to know now, so we don't waste any time on palace intrigue."

Talia was the first to find words. "What—how—I mean, who's going to handle operations?"

"I don't know."

"Blimey," said Michael. "That's a lot to take in. Without Steve, we could lose whatever momentum we still have."

David let them process the news at their own pace. He

Jonah

answered their questions as patiently as he could. When the shock waves finally dissipated, he asked them to think about a replacement.

Back in his office, he heard a knock at his door. He steeled himself for another bout with Steve. It was Raven.

"May I come in?" she said quietly.

David waved her to a seat.

"Listen, David. I know you're upset. Firing Steve couldn't have been the most pleasant task in the world. I just wanted you to know, I think you made the right decision."

Now it was David's turn to be stunned. This was Raven, Steve's professional soulmate.

"Steve hasn't been happy for a long time. I won't go into his personal life, but he's never recovered from being passed over by Andy. This whole strategic exercise was the last straw. He doesn't like change, and being asked to reinvent the company was like being asked to dig his own grave. He couldn't see a role for himself. It's not your fault."

"Thanks, Raven. That means a lot to me. How about you? How are you feeling?"

"I have to say, I had serious misgivings. My whole career has been selling beds in hotels. I had to remind myself that my job is bigger than that. I'm not just selling beds, I'm selling experiences. I'm selling adventure and personal growth."

Inside, David beamed. "I have to say, Raven, I was really thrilled about your call center insight. That was first-rate creative thinking."

"It's funny," she said. "I always thought creativity was for other people. You were either born with it or you weren't. And I knew I wasn't. My strength is rational, logical, step-by-step productivity. That's where I'm on solid ground."

"What changed?"

"Nothing. I just used Cultura's rational process for applying your imagination. Now I get it. Creative thinking isn't a special gift. It just takes work and a willingness to embrace a different approach."

"So you're on board?"

"I'm on board."

David stood up and did something he never thought he would. He hugged her.

28

SWARMING

Tuesday, December 28. David asked the BigSky team members to arrive a half-hour early to share their thoughts on filling Steve's position. Everyone seemed to be in a much better mood. Michael and Yasemin were particularly sanguine—both admitted feeling a touch of relief at Steve's leaving.

For the most part, the suggestions for replacing him involved various search methods: They could network with executives they already knew. They could post a job description on LinkedIn. Or they could turn the listing over to a search firm, as they'd done in the past. But Talia had a different idea.

"What about Ernesto?" she said.

"Ernesto Martinez?" said David. "Steve's assistant? He seems so young."

"Like someone else we know?" said Talia, unable to hide a smile. "Listen, Ernesto has been helping Steve for three years now, and he's been doing a lot of the work himself."

"That's right," said Raven. "He has a hospitality degree from Cornell, speaks several languages, and has great rapport with the employees. They respect him. They say he's fair and firm—they always know where they stand with Ernesto. Plus," she said, "he's a really nice guy."

"I don't know. Seems like a long shot. But I'll meet with him before we announce Steve's departure."

The Cultura crew joined the group at 9:00. Gard scanned the room to gauge the extent of the damage. "Everyone okay?" His question was met with a mixture of nods and shrugs.

"We're a little unsure about the future of operations," said Raven. "We can't decide if the glass is half empty or—"

"Ah!" said Shigeru, the Zen master. "People who wonder whether the glass is half empty or half full are missing the point." He held his index finger in the air. "The glass is refillable."

"True," said David with a grin. "On that note, let's get down to business. Gard, what do you have for us today?"

Gard walked to the whiteboard. "After three weeks of work, I feel like we've finally got a bead on the strategy. Does everyone agree?"

They said they did.

"Okay. What we need now is to start building out the experience. The board will need a more complete story about what the new business will look like, smell like, taste like. It's not their job to imagine how people will engage with our website. It's our job."

Vigorous nods.

"And the best way to get it done is with this." He reached for a marker and wrote *S-W-A-R-M-I-N-G*. "Has anyone heard of it?"

They said they hadn't.

"Shigeru, would you like to explain?"

"Sure. The idea of swarming comes from the military. It's the concept of attacking an enemy—our project, in this case—from all sides at once." He explained that too many strategy teams fetishize the usual tools—SWOT analyses, financial modeling, consumer studies, market scans, landscape analyses—as if they held magical powers. They then apply these tools in a rigid linear sequence.

"Truthfully, Cultura wasn't much different in the old days," he admitted. "We'd line up strategy tasks as if they were railway cars on a track. First, the executive team would define the goals. The analysts would assess the company's strengths, weaknesses, opportunities, and threats. Next came market researchers to size up the market and the competitive landscape. Then we'd take that information and craft a plan. The plan would go to the various teams for execution, and the final products or services would go to market. It was a linear process—*A*, *B*, *C*, *D*, etc. Do you follow?"

They did.

"Do you see the problem?"

They didn't.

"Okay. The problem was, once step A was completed, step B was powerless to change it. For all intents and purposes, that door was closed—it was a one-way track. By the time you got to E or F, the resulting strategy was unrelated to the original goals, or so watered-down that it was too weak to do the job. Like that children's game, Telephone. You know the one?"

Michael raised his hand. "In the UK we called it 'Whispering Down the Lane.' One person whispers a phrase to another person, who quickly whispers it to another person, and so on down the lane, until the last person hears something completely different to the original phrase."

"Same game. That's the problem we now have with traditional strategy. It worked all right in a more predictable time, but it doesn't work in an era of hyper-complexity and rapid change."

Yasemin spoke up. "Are you saying we shouldn't use a process?"

"In a way, yes. Let me ask you something, Yaz. You're an accomplished designer. When you design something—let's say an interior space or a piece of furniture or a garden for one of your hotels—how do you go about your work? Do you start with research, then move to sketches, then turn the sketches into models, then execute the final design—*A, B, C, D*?"

Yasemin blushed. "Well, not really. I mean, that's what I tell everybody." She looked over at David sheepishly. "I might start with sketches, then realize I need to do some research, then try a model, then end up doing more sketches. It's more like *B, A, C, B, C, D*. Or maybe *A, B, Z, R, Q, R, D*. It all depends on what I learn from each step. There's no set order."

"Would you also say that your actual process is somewhat wasteful, untidy, random, unconscious, and unpredictable?"

She shrugged. "It can be."

"Somewhat wasteful, for sure. But very right. Your work looks great. It drives business. It delivers profits. It wins awards. Every innovator from the dawn of time has used the same unpredictable process. So why don't we just admit that it works and use the same 'no-process process' in our teams? Anybody?"

"I'm not a designer," said Talia. "But wouldn't you have chaos? Teamwork needs to be organized so people don't keep bumping into each other. Doesn't it?"

"That's the conventional wisdom, yes. But what if bumping into each other is not a flaw but a feature? What if the 'bumps' are what create the new ideas? After all, that's pretty much what happens in an individual brain. Ideas bump into other ideas and trigger new ideas. Without the bumps, there'd be no surprises—and no new ideas."

Raven raised her hand. "At our session on Christmas Day, I started with the assumption that people in call centers are poorly paid. Then I reversed it. I said, what if they were highly paid? These two conflicting ideas bumped into each other, which led me to a third idea. Is that what you mean?"

"Exactly!"

Raven looked pleased.

"Now, what if we could simulate that single-brain process in a multi-brained team? What if all the different thoughts, notions, insights, and perspectives of a group were allowed to crash into one another in some productive way? Wouldn't it be like creative thinking times ten?"

They nodded.

"That's the theory behind swarming."

David spoke up. "I think the reason we never did that at Sestina was that our clients wouldn't know what they were getting, or when, and we wouldn't know how to estimate our time or costs. Without a clearly delineated process, we might not have gotten any projects to begin with."

"You're assuming there's no other kind of process. It's true that creative collaboration—whether for strategy, product design, decision-making—needs a process. But not necessarily a stiff, linear one. It needs to be elastic, so it can respond to the real needs of exploration."

Gard jumped in. "We've already done the linear work. We know why we're in business, who our customers are, where we're going to compete, and how we're going to win. Now we need to explore the *what*. What the hell are we selling?"

"We're selling an online service," said David.

"Sure," said Gard. "But what does it look like? What are its features? How does it work? The board will need answers to these questions before they can give us the green light.

"Here's what I'm proposing," he continued. "Let's recruit a few of the missing functions our team's brain will need. Let's bring in Cultura's graphic designer, Bel Hartfield, for the presentation, and Dayna Redpath for copywriting and naming. Let's pull in the Thompson Twins from the outside to help us prototype the website."

"The Thompson Twins?" said David.

"Don't laugh," said Cary. "They're amazing."

"Can you get them here tomorrow?"

"They're already booked," said Gard.

Swarming

* * *

A young man with straight, dark hair sat opposite David in the small conference room outside his office. He didn't seem much older than twenty, but David knew he was closer to thirty. He had perfect posture and an air of calm energy.

"Ernesto, we don't know each other well, but I've heard good things about your performance here."

"Thank you, sir."

"Can you tell me a little about your job?"

"I assist Steve Cochran in operations. I follow up on all of his projects, making sure the various processes and programs stay on track. I'm involved in training, hiring, and sometimes firing. I fill in for Steve whenever he's out," he said, pausing, "which has been more and more lately."

"You mean because of his strategy commitments?"

Ernesto looked down. "And other things. I can pretty much do the same tasks he does."

"Where is he when he's out?"

"I don't always know, sir. It hasn't been a problem. I've got everything under control."

David paused. "Ernesto, how would you like to run operations yourself, on a temporary basis?"

He looked confused. "Where's Mr. Cochran?"

"I'm sorry to tell you, Ernesto, Mr. Cochran is no longer with the company."

His dark eyes widened. "Is he all right?"

"He's fine. Can you do it?"

Ernesto's smile grew, filling his fresh, youthful face.

29

MISSION

Wednesday, December 29. David sat at the breakfast table with a copy of the *Wall Street Journal*, his coffee growing cold on the side. He stared with disbelief at a one-column piece on page seven of "Business & Finance." A portrait of Steve was at the top.

> ### BigSky Faces Gathering Storm
> By NATHAN TENEBRI
>
> NEW YORK, NY—Stephen J. Cochran, BigSky's chief of operations, was summarily fired yesterday in the midst of a reported turnaround effort. The company has faced shrinking revenues for four straight quarters, resisting CEO David Stone's efforts to reverse the decline. Mr. Cochran had been with company for six years, during which time BigSky's revenues had grown steadily. After Mr. Stone took the reins from founder Andrew Vineyard, revenues began to plummet. BigSky's stock price, as of yesterday, was down 33 percent from last year. No reason was given for Mr. Cochran's termination.

Summarily fired? No reason was given? How did they know about it in the first place? BigSky hadn't released an announcement. If it was Steve who had leaked it, he was violating his confidentiality

Mission

agreement, putting his severance package at risk.

The article's innuendo was clear. The company was doing well before David took over. After failing repeatedly, he terminated one of the leaders responsible for the company's success. To make matter worse, the company appeared to go dark on the subject.

He called PR to find out what had happened. They didn't know, but would look into it. Next, he called Andy to prepare him for the blowback. There was no answer, so he sent him a text asking for a quick meeting. Then he placed a call to investor relations to give them a heads-up.

This was the last thing he needed today. The new team members were expected in forty minutes. With only a week until the presentation, he wanted to set the stage for the remaining work. He emailed the team, saying to start without him. His phone clattered on the table.

"David, what's going on?"

"Andy, thanks. Listen, I'm sorry I didn't tell you about Steve earlier. I had it on my calendar to call you this morning. The *Journal* article hit before I could get to it."

Andy exhaled loudly. "Our annual meeting is three weeks from now, and with the shareholders on the warpath…" He left his thought hanging. "What exactly happened?"

David explained the situation, starting with Steve's negative attitude in the strategy sessions, and ending with his meltdown on Monday.

"I see. You know Steve and Raven were my go-to people before you came on."

"I know."

"How's Raven?"

"Great. She had trouble adjusting to the strategy work at first, but she's coming around. She agreed that Steve needed to go."

"Who'll replace him?"

"I'm giving Ernesto Martinez a shot."

Andy thought about this. "Good. But keep me informed from now on. I have one thing in common with the Godfather—I like to hear bad news right away."

"Sorry, I promise."

When they hung up, David reflected on Andy's reaction. He seemed calm, almost as if he was enjoying himself. The Godfather?

He entered the war room just before 11:00. The whiteboard was covered with notes and diagrams outlining the mission. On the right side was a list of tasks and responsibilities.

Gard introduced David to the new team members. "David, meet Bel Hartfield. Bel works as a graphic designer at Cultura. She'll be putting together the slideshow and any graphics we'll need along the way." David shook her hand. Her palm was lightly calloused, like a gardener's.

"And this is Dayna Redpath," he said, adding, "our ace copywriter. She'll write the text for the presentation and also help with naming."

"Glad you could join us," said David.

"And these two are the Thompsons: Aduwa and Braley." David had noticed the "twins" the moment he walked in. They were as different as two people could be. Aduwa was small and stocky with blue-black skin and sparkling black hair. She wore a men's white dress shirt with the collar turned up and a pair of distressed jeans.

Braley was tall and thin with blue-white skin and floppy red hair. He wore black knee-high boots, gray tights, a charcoal kilt, and two thin black sweaters, one with a collar, one without.

"As you can see," said Gard, "they're not really twins."

Everyone laughed at David's expression.

Mission

"We just like working together," explained Aduwa, her smile a suddenly-switched-on lightbulb.

"Braley is a programmer from San Francisco, not far from our shop," said Gard, "and Addie is a web designer from Lagos. She's here on an H1-B visa, so we may not have her that long. Bull is cracking down on countries like Nigeria."

David gave her a look of apology.

She shrugged as if to say, "That's life."

"We'll be using the twins for prototyping. The actual website, going forward, will end up with a much larger group."

Gard took David through the assignments. They were purposely left loose for the first day, allowing the members to work on aspects of the brand that interested them. They'd get more precise later.

"The schedule looks like this," he said, pointing to the board. "Today we'll work on our own, making notes and sketches for possible features, experiences, look-and-feel issues, and so forth. We can share back and forth as we come up with ideas. Tomorrow we'll get more specific with actual touchpoints."

"Touchpoints?" said David.

"The places where customers come in contact with the brand. The website, of course, but everything that surrounds it too— graphics, nomenclature, advertising, social messaging, and whatever else we can think of." He paused for a moment. "Tomorrow is Friday, New Year's Eve."

"I'd like us work through the weekend. Sorry."

"Okay, we figured that. We'll use tomorrow to assess our ideas and decide the best direction for the pitch. At that point, we'll know better how to spend the rest of our time. Can you and I have a brief chat?"

They walked to an unoccupied meeting room and closed the door.

"I think it's going well," said Gard. "Steve's out of the picture, the new people are comfy, everyone else is working together like old hands. I think you can take it from here. Shig will cover for me, and Cary can stay and help with research. She's single, so getting back isn't so urgent for her. I miss my kids. My wife is probably browsing Tinder by now. My fucking clients think I've absconded with their advances. Shit, sorry. Anyway, a resourceful farm boy like you? You'll be fine."

"Of course I will. I have to tell you, Gard, I've learned a heck of a lot in the last few weeks. I knew you'd save my bacon, but I had no idea I'd be getting a master's degree in brand strategy. I can't tell you how grateful I am."

"Hey, it's not the first time I've saved your skinny ass. How about all those pitches I pulled into the strike zone? No wonder the umps had it in for you." He grinned, stood up, and opened his arms. David gave him a long hug.

"I mean it, man. Thanks."

"Whoa, don't go all mushy on me. Get back to work and make me proud. Like the old Slingshot."

Gard said his goodbyes and quickly disappeared. David checked his phone. There was a voicemail from PR saying that no one from the *Journal* had called for comment. The information must have come from somewhere else.

Corporate communications had been working on an announcement about Steve's departure, and needed David's approval before sending it out. It would simply say that Steve and BigSky had parted over differences on strategic direction.

The HR people had done some research and found mysterious gaps in his schedule. They recommended against addressing these, since David had never spoken to Steve about them before. But they promised to call and warn him if they discovered Steve had violated his agreement.

David realized that the announcement was unlikely to quell the curiosity. Investors would want to know more about these

Mission

so-called differences on direction, and what had triggered the firing. Was it David's fault? Had he gone too far off the reservation for Steve's sensibilities? Was he an immature leader who tried to micromanage his more seasoned staffers? Was he trying to blame others for his own mistakes?

David knew that if Steve had found a journalist eager to make a reputation, one article was only the beginning. He thought about calling Steve directly, but a move like that could complicate things. Probably wiser to wait and see how the situation played out.

At 4:10 he walked back to the war room and found the group engaged in animated conversation. When they finally noticed he was there, they waved him over.

"David," said Michael, "we've been having the most interesting discussion with Cary and the twins. It's about how recommendation engines create reinforcing behavioral loops."

"Explain," said David.

Michael nodded to Aduwa.

"Let's say," she said, "you go to a website and make some choices. An algorithm uses those choices to propose other choices it thinks you'll like. It so happens, you do. So the algorithm gives you more of them. Every time an algorithm gives you what you want, it narrows your world. It's programmed only for your immediate satisfaction."

"Sounds logical. Is that bad?"

"Yes, because it conflicts with two of our goals. First, we want our customers to continually open up to new experiences, not just the same-old, same-old, ad infinitum. Second, we want to continually expand our tribe. If everyone lives in their own little world, they're less likely to form a strong community around our brand."

"This observation comes from a guy named Eli Pariser," said

Cary. "He calls it the *you-loop*. It's like a house of mirrors, where every place you look you only see yourself."

David's nightmare from earlier in the month, in which he was trapped in a cage, surrounded only by images of himself, flashed before his eyes. It had been a signal that his life was too constricted, a choice he had made when he threw himself into his work. How much better he felt after opening up his circle.

"What can we do about it?" he said.

"Aduwa," said Michael, "tell David your idea."

"I thought we could create 'wild cards' to break the house-of-mirrors effect. We could build in little features that would surprise people and wake them up to a larger world of travel choices."

"What kind of features?"

"Dunno," she said. "How much time do we have?"

"Six days."

Aduwa's smile lit up the whole room. "That's all it took for the good Lord to create the whole universe."

30

TOUCHPOINTS

Thursday, December 30. The Magnificent Eleven, as Cary called the remaining team members, were back in the war room at 8:00 a.m. David had asked them to come in early for the next six days. "The good Lord," he explained, "had an advantage we don't have."

"Yeah," said Cary, "that whole supernatural thing."

"And great hair," said Michael, staring pointedly at Cary's unruly mop. She responded with narrowed eyes and pursed lips.

Shigeru stood up and walked to the front. "I suggest we work together in the war room as much as possible today. At this stage, we want as much cross-pollination as we can get—those ideas bumping up against each other. Go ahead and form smaller teams as needed, and by all means check in with the teams whose work needs to dovetail with yours, or whose work might inspire yours. Any questions?"

They shook their heads.

"One more thing," he said. "As you invent your touchpoints, remember to use the brand framework as a filter. Every touchpoint should be a fractal of the larger brand."

"A fractal?" asked Talia.

"I know what that is," said Yasemin. "Have you ever looked at the veins of a leaf?"

"Sure."

"The veins grow out from the stalk like branches on a tree, right? If you look closely at the veins, you can see smaller veins coming out from those, and so on, smaller and smaller. A leaf looks like a miniature tree, and the veins look like miniature branches. That's one example of a fractal, but you can find fractals all over nature."

"And that's like branding?" said Talia.

"In a perfect world it is," said Shigeru. "Each expression of the brand should be the brand in miniature. No touchpoint should contradict our onlyness. Think of it as arranging messages on stacked levels, from the highest level down to the lowest level."

Talia looked over at Michael with round, innocent eyes. "What would Shakespeare say?"

Michael tilted his head. "Methinks thou doth mocketh me."

Talia pouted, pretending innocence.

"I know you're being funny, fair Talia, but I actually have a serious answer for you."

"Okay, let's hear it."

"The thing that made Shakespeare so successful was that he wrote his plays for a tiered audience."

"A what?"

"A tiered audience. He tried to please the widest range of people possible, from the royals up high in the box seats to the groundlings down on the theater floor, standing in the sawdust, pissing out their ale between pints."

"Gross," said Talia.

"The point is, he was telling the same story to various people at various levels. The royals came for the history lesson, and the punters came for the dirty jokes."

"You're planning to tell dirty jokes now?"

"Don't be cheeky."

"Michael's right," said Shigeru. "Building a brand is a like writing a play—a never-ending play that customers choose to act out. It's our job to create the characters, the props, the trajectory of the plot. The customers' job is to tell the stories. Remember, the brand isn't what *we* say it is."

"It's what *they* say it is," said the members in unison.

Shigeru laughed. "Shall we get to work?"

David and Yasemin joined the Thompson Twins on website design. Talia and Dayna teamed up to tackle the tiered stories that Michael had described. Michael and Cary set about creating messaging for the home page. Raven and Shigeru took a crack at writing a sample press release to announce the product. Bel moved from team to team to bring a visual sensibility to their ideas.

After about an hour, Cary rose to her feet. "Ahem!" she said, waiting for heads to bob up. "*Ahem!*" They finally stopped talking and turned to face her. "It seems nobody wants to address the elephant in the room." A few members scanned the room, as if they might be able to see it. "The elephant in the room is that we have no name."

"That's right!" said David. "I guess I figured a name was one of the less urgent items on the list."

"It is. But we should have something semi-realistic to use as a placeholder. 'Newco' doesn't cut it."

David said, "Okay. Anybody?"

"Compass dot com?" offered Dayna.

"True North," said Michael.

Talia shouted: "Travel Ho!"

"Back of Beyond," offered Shigeru.

"*Camino*," came a voice from the doorway. They turned to see who belonged to it.

"Ernesto!" said David. "Come in for a second. Everybody, say hi to our new temporary COO, Ernesto Martinez." They welcomed him with handshakes and warm congratulations.

"*Camino* is Spanish for *way*," said Ernesto. "We could say our website is the new way to build a trip."

"Build a trip," repeated Dayna. "How about TripBuilder?"

"TripBuilder!" said David. "That should work. *Muchas gracias por la idea, señor.*"

"*Vaya con Dios*," said Ernesto, with a two-fingered wave.

The real elephant, thought David, had been Steve. The team seemed to be working much better without the black-hatter-in-chief casting a pall on the proceedings. Steve had trouble contributing anything worthwhile in a month of meetings, whereas Ernesto tossed out a helpful suggestion on his way to the men's room.

David suddenly remembered to check his phone. He found a voicemail from Patricia in PR. More leaks from Steve?

"Patti, what's going on?"

"The *Wall Street Journal* is working on another story. They're asking for a comment."

"What about?"

"Apparently, they know something about our plans. They're

running an article on Monday, January 3."

"Jesus H.," he said, dropping his head.

"Sorry, Mr. Stone."

"It's not your fault, Patti. Give me the contact info."

He hurried back to the war room and motioned for Raven and Michael to meet him outside. He walked them to the smaller conference room and closed the door.

"Listen, guys. It's the *Journal* again. They're planning to run a story about our new business."

"What?" said Raven. "We don't even have a new business."

"Somebody must have leaked."

"Steve," said Michael through clenched teeth.

"We don't know for sure if it was Steve. It could have been anyone, even somebody from the board. The question is: What should we do about it?"

Raven knitted her brow. "We were just talking about how a brand is a kind of story. The problem here is the arc. Right now the story is negative, right? BigSky is in trouble. A young, immature—sorry, David—inexperienced CEO tanks on his first big-league outing. It's tempting for the press to cast your next move in the same light."

"I see what you mean. Young CEO makes one more bonehead play in a long line of bonehead plays. The *Journal* looks superior and smart while profiting from their little scoop."

"Something like that," said Raven.

Michael's neck pulsed. "I had more respect for the *Journal* before News Corp got hold of it. It had gravitas. The stories were balanced and the headlines restrained. They've turned it into a shrieking rag."

"Maybe so," said Raven. "But let's imagine what kind of comment might bend the arc. What if you said we were setting out to change the history of travel?"

"*That's* pretty bold," said Michael with a tinge of apprehension.

"Well, aren't we?" said Raven.

"So we are," admitted David. "That'd certainly raise the stakes. Still, if we pointed to the centerfield fence like Babe Ruth, then whiffed, we'd look like fools, and the original story would be confirmed."

"Yes, but wouldn't it be confirmed anyway? The cat's out of the bag. If we play innocent now, or just refuse to comment, speculation will ratchet up. On the other hand, if we give them a bigger, more tantalizing scoop, we'll cut the legs out from under the leaker. Shig and I wrote a sample press release with some good ideas in it. You can riff off that. It might be our best bet."

David had to admire Raven's ability to connect the dots. He thanked her and went to his office to call Andy.

"It's your problem, David," said Andy, after listening patiently. "I can't help you. You'll have to work it out for yourself."

It dawned on him that the Cultura folks were more correct than he'd imagined. The public, not the company, tells the story. He called the reporter at the *Journal* with a half-written press release trembling in his hand. Here it was. Their very first touchpoint.

31

FIREWORKS

Friday, December 31. Sokrates weaved the Prius through the light morning traffic in Chelsea. The last day of the year was clear and unseasonably warm. David felt in need of a little "Sok time," as he put it in his text.

"Slave driver!" said Sokrates. "You're actually making people work on New Year's Eve?"

"We're down to less than a week. It's do or die."

"I remember when you first told me about this fire drill. Seems like a year ago. But I guess it's going."

"It's going, but it's getting complicated." He told Sokrates about firing Steve, and about the *Journal* article that broke without any help from BigSky.

"Yeah, I saw that little hit piece. Made you look like Richard Bull, blaming other people for your own mistakes."

"Thanks for that."

"Just sayin'."

"They're running another article on Monday."

"Lordy."

"This time they asked me for a comment."

"What'd you say?"

"I told them we were reinventing the travel industry."

"Whoa. How you gonna do that?"

"With an automated trip planner. But that's just between you and me. We still have to build it."

Sokrates paused for a second. "Tell me if I've got this right. You're hoping to upend the industry by disintermediating travel agents?"

"Right."

"So you're not only taking on the agency business, but the whole travel ecosystem?"

"Right."

"And you have to convince a bunch of tight-ass, tradition-bound hotel tycoons to go along with it?"

"Right."

"You've got more balls than a pachinko machine."

David sighed. "Any advice?"

"Let me ask you this: Is there one thing you could tell the directors—anything at all—that would force them to fund the project?"

"Force them? I'm not sure about that. We're working on it.

We've still got five days."

"Happy New Year!" he yelled, adding a long honk of the horn.

"Very funny."

The team shifted into high gear. Sticky notes littered the whiteboard. Sketches, screenshots, and wireframe diagrams fought for wall space. As David entered the room, Shigeru was making a list on a large easel pad.

"Okay," he said, "we've got 'information' and 'entertainment.' What other motives would people have for using TripBuilder?"

"Self-enhancement," said Bel. "Being in the know. Being a better traveler."

He wrote these down. "What else?"

Michael raised his hand. "Social enhancement. Being recognized as an expert. Having status within the group."

"Just plain social engagement," said Braley. "People sharing their experiences."

"And developing friendships around their interests," said Aduwa.

"Anything else?" said Shigeru. He looked around. "No? Okay, let's see what we have. Cary, can you place these in order of importance?"

"Clearly," she said, "social enhancement is first and foremost. Humans are social animals, and the pecking order within a group is key. 'My tattoo is cooler than yours'—that sort of thing. Next would be simple social engagement. Then, I would say, self-enhancement. I'd put entertainment and information last."

"Your order seems like the opposite of what most would say."

"I'm looking at it like an anthropologist. We're trying to build a tribe, right?"

"Right," said Shigeru. "Why don't we do a yellow-hat exercise. Let's make a list of all the things the tribe might go for."

As they shouted out their ideas, Shigeru jotted them down.

"Customer reviews," said Talia.

"Composite reviews," said Aduwa, "averaged from existing review sites."

"Good."

"How about twenty-four-hour live help," said Braley, "in case you get thrown in jail, or your wallet goes missing."

"Or both," said Cary.

"How about humorous on-hold messages," said Michael, "while we locate a good lawyer for you."

"Total trip insurance," volunteered Talia. "Covering everything, not just your flights. If we had a big enough pool, the cost of premiums would be reasonable."

"Travel stories," said Cary. "People love to talk about their adventures. Why not capture those stories in travel-writing competitions?"

"Photography competitions," added Bel. "We could hand out awards, or free trips, for winning photos."

"Why not have a food section?" said Braley. "Chefs from various hotels and restaurants could share their best recipes."

"Seconded," said David.

"How about world music compilations?" said Yasemin. "We could market those right on the site."

"A dedicated YouTube channel," suggested Aduwa.

"Annual travel conference," said Raven.

At eight o'clock that evening, five boxes of pizza arrived from Capizzi, along with five bottles of champagne from Veritas. They'd be working until midnight or later. David figured there was no reason they shouldn't celebrate the new year along with the rest of the city. Down on the streets below, revelers were already streaming toward Times Square for the countdown party.

"Dinner gong!" chimed Talia. She and Michael had placed two tables end to end, and arranged the dishes and flatware. The team members gathered around the tables and grabbed slices of prosciutto with arugula, soppressata with sun-dried tomatoes, roasted asparagus with truffle oil. They talked excitedly about travel, food, politics, and their New Year's resolutions.

"My resolution," said Michael, "is to work a lot less."

"Mine too," said Talia. "My husband has already joined a bowling league. He doesn't even like bowling."

"My wife keeps a framed photo of my face on my pillow," said Shigeru. "She's afraid she won't recognize me when I get home." As proof, he passed around his iPhone showing the photo.

"In that case we've got a conflict," said David. "My New Year's resolution is to get you all to work *more*."

Shigeru crumpled up a napkin and threw it at David, who batted it away. Others followed until the room was maelstrom of napkin balls. After a few minutes, they picked up their napkins, cleared the dishes, and went back to work.

By 9:30 they had separated into various offices, working intensely in twos and threes. David made the rounds to check their progress. Walking past a smaller office, he overheard Raven and Michael.

"Do you really trust David to pull this off?" said Michael, sounding tired. "I'm beginning to think this whole thing is a mirage. When it's over, we'll all be out of jobs and wishing we'd worked on our résumés. I care about David a lot, but I'm not sure he cares about us—for him, it's the mission."

"It's our mission too," said Raven. "David's a mensch. How many people do you know who would stand up to a stuffy board of directors and try to change the course of an industry? The least we can do—the very least—is to help him do it."

"And if we fail?"

"We fail together."

David slipped away and walked toward a cubicle where Cary was sitting, working on her laptop. She jumped when she realized he was standing behind her. She reached over and pulled up a chair. "How's your father doing?"

"My father? How did you know about that?"

"Tally overheard your call on Christmas Eve."

David shook his head. "He's doing much better, thanks. He's home. His voice is coming back."

"David, this may seem out of line, but I wanted to tell you something."

"What?"

"I know you."

He cocked his head. "What do you mean?"

"I know who you are. I grew up in Portland. My father and I used to drive up to the Rainier games. I remember the scandal. I checked with Gard and found out you're the same David Stone."

His brows knitted. "That was a long time ago, Cary."

"I know. I just wanted to say I was disappointed when you dropped out. The guy had it coming. Things like that happen all the time in baseball."

"You're a fan?"

"I like a good game. Listen, I think you're an exceptional CEO, and I've worked with quite a few. Don't give up this time. And don't let your team give up."

Fifteen minutes before midnight, David gathered the group together in the war room. The champagne sat chilling in a plastic maintenance bucket in the corner. He could detect signs of exhaustion in the team members' faces and body language.

"Thanks, everyone," he said, looking around the room. "It's almost midnight on the last day of the year. In fact, the last day of the toughest year in BigSky's history. I know it's been hard on you. But," he said, holding up his thumb and forefinger, "we are *that* close to winning our first major battle. I can feel it. And I have to say I'm incredibly proud of you. And proud of the work we're doing together.

"The service we're building is more than a fancy utility designed to bring in revenues. It's a mechanism for igniting awe, curiosity, and a sense of adventure. It's a force opposing everything narrow-minded, shallow, and selfish in the world. When we finally win, when we overcome the obstacles and alter the course of travel, we're going to look back and mark *this* as the day when everything changed—the day we gelled, the moment we knew that this year would be our year."

The twins passed out flutes of champagne. Cary held hers in both hands, standing still in the back of the room.

"I'd like to propose a toast," David said, raising a glass as if it were a shimmering sword. "To our mission, and to the most creative, courageous team this side of the Hudson."

They cheered loudly and clinked glasses. Outside they could hear the crowd beginning to chant, "Ten, nine, eight…"

Michael leapt onto the table and held his glass out. "If we are marked to die, we are enough to do our country loss; and if to live, the fewer men, the greater share of honor."

"Five, four, three…"

"We few, we happy few, we band of brothers…"

Horns blared and fireworks cracked the midnight sky. They gazed out at the giant ULL, the flashing lights of Times Square reflecting off the gold-tinted glass. It looked as if the Bull Building were exploding and might be reduced to a pile of shards in seconds.

David glanced over and saw Cary, colored flashes of light playing softly on her features. Her hair, freed from the bondage of her barrette, was now hanging sweetly over one eye. He wondered why he hadn't noticed how pretty she was.

Without warning she ran up and threw her arms around his

neck, pressing her body against his. She kissed him. An electric current sizzled down his spine. *No, no, no. This can't happen.* He looked around, embarrassed, but saw others hugging and kissing in the pyrotechnic light.

Talia went to a computer and turned on Spotify. They spent the next hour dancing, laughing, and drinking champagne. David finally shooed them home, telling them to take "a whole hour off" in the morning.

"Our hero," said Cary, without a trace of irony.

32

SCRAMBLE

Saturday, January 1. The team straggled into the war room between 9:00 and 9:30 on the first day of the year, heads hurting but spirits willing—"bloody but unbowed," as Michael put it.

On the street below were scores of revelers, ragged and drunk, who had refused to stop celebrating. They milled around a large crane anchored outside the Bull Building, an oversize letter *B* dangling from its cable. Bull would never allow his vaunted logo to remain defaced into the new year.

David thought about what Sokrates had said: *Is there one thing you could tell the directors—anything at all—that would force them to fund the project?*

It had to be there. But where? He only hoped it would show up in the next few days. In the meantime, they still had to prototype the website's feature set, develop messaging, and refine the revenue model for the business itself.

Shigeru recommended they use an approach called a *scramble.*

Scramble

"The concept comes from golf," he said, grabbing a marker. "It's a tournament format where everyone on the team hits a ball off the tee, like this." He drew four lines fanning out from a point. "The captain chooses the best shot." He circled the end point of one of the lines. "The players hit their next ball from here. They repeat this routine until one of them sinks a putt:"

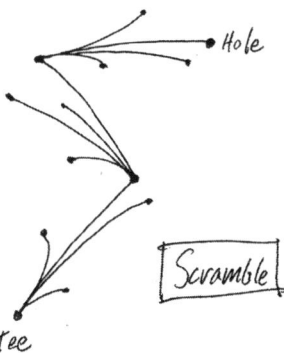

"In a creative scramble, everyone takes their best shot at one feature or element of the brand offering. The co-captains, David and I, will make the call on which of the ideas are the most promising. Then everyone will go back and redesign their elements to align better with the selected ones. With each round, the various elements get more interesting. New ideas surface. Alternative directions come into focus. Make sense so far?"

"Where'd you get this idea?" said Braley. "It sounds like agile software development."

"It's similar. It's based on a theory called *set-based decision making* that allows teams to explore multiple pathways without a clear idea of where they'll end up. You go in not knowing, so you come out knowing. It's part of our overall approach to *agile strategy*." He wrote the words on the whiteboard.

"The key elements of agile strategy," he said, "are the five *Q*s of strategy, the five Ps of design thinking, and collaborative techniques like scrambles and swarms. A scramble keeps you from going too far down a single path and having to retrace your steps."

"That concept isn't much of a stretch for us," said Aduwa, looking at Braley.

"Yup. We get it," he said.

"Then I think we're in a good position to choose the basic elements we need to prototype. I'll start making a list and let's see if we agree." He turned toward the board and began writing:

> Name
> Trademark
> Home page design
> Feature set
> Revenue model
> Levels of engagement
> Top-line messaging
> Collateral pieces

"Anything else?" said Shigeru, looking around for volunteers.

"What do you mean 'levels of engagement'?" asked Raven.

"That's from Michael's insight about Shakespeare. The idea that we can reach a larger audience, create a richer experience, by offering different tiers of engagement."

"Hmm." Raven pulled on her lower lip. "It seems to me that the various levels of engagement could align with the revenue and pricing models."

"Maybe," said Shigeru. "Why don't you, Talia, and Michael work on those two items as a team?"

"The name and logo could be created together too," said Dayna. "Bel and I could team up on those."

"Good idea," said Bel. "Some names make for better visuals than others. It might help to see how they would look before set-

Scramble

tling on a final name."

"Cary," said Shigeru, "I think you should lead the naming exercise and vet the names for legal issues as you go. Remember, we don't need final elements for anything, so don't worry about finding the perfect name. All we can do is our best in the time we have available. Addie, you and Braley can tackle the feature set."

"We can work on the home page at the same time," said Aduwa.

Braley agreed. "Is it possible to get sample text to work with?"

"I'll start writing as soon as we complete the name and trademark work," said Dayna. "For now, just throw in some *Lorem ipsum* and set TripBuilder in Helvetica." The twins nodded.

"Yaz," said Shigeru, "I thought you could work with the twins to provide imagery and aesthetic guidance for the home page, and on the secondary pages, too, if we get that far."

"I have some ideas," she said.

"Bel," he said, "maybe when you get done with the logo, you can think about collateral elements."

"Like what?"

"No idea. I'm sure you'll have some thoughts as the work progresses. David, you and I can move from group to group and offer help or supervision where needed."

David agreed.

"Cary, how else can we use your research skills?"

"I can pull some info on best practices, worst practices, and the habits and needs of our tribe. I can also start testing our concepts and prototypes as soon as they're ready."

"Okay," said Shigeru, clapping his hands. "Let's scramble."

David retreated to his office to address some urgent emails. As he worked, he grew aware of a noise coming from down on the street. It sounded like chanting. He looked up from his laptop and saw a man climbing the lattice-like arm of the crane across the street. He wore a backpack and used a lineman's belt as a climbing aid. He'd reached the jib of the crane, the part that allows the boom to extend.

On a platform at the base of the Bull logo, three installers were working on the sign. They'd wrestled the giant *B* to the wall, and were now cinching it to the steel grid. Most of its weight was still supported by the crane.

At first, David thought the climber was a member of the crew, but the three signage workers were dressed in orange jackets, while the climber was dressed in black and wore a ski mask. David went to the window and looked down. The crowd of revelers had transformed itself into a pulsing mob of protesters. The police had cordoned off the area around the crane. The crowd was surging up against it, threatening to break through. He couldn't read the posters, but he could make out the chant: "Keep oil out! Keep oil out!" Sirens howled in the distance.

He went back to his laptop and logged onto the *New York Times*. He found the story on the home page. Over the holiday, Richard Bull had signed an executive order allowing oil drilling in Everglades National Park.

Dear God, thought David. There were endangered species there, not to mention important sources of drinking water. What if a hurricane or some other event damaged the drilling operation? He imagined a nightmare scenario of oil-drenched manatees, turtles, and Great Blue Herons writhing helplessly on the shore. The ecosystem might never recover.

The climber was closing in on the platform. The workers began detaching the giant letter *B*. They couldn't risk the large metal structure breaking loose and falling onto the crowd: they'd have to lower both the letterform and the climber together.

A bullhorn sounded from the street below. "This is the police.

Do not move. Stop climbing. *Immediately.*" A rescue team had jockeyed a truck with a suicide net into place down on the street. Media crews transmitted live coverage as the events unfolded.

The man in black swung himself over the rail and elbowed one of the workers out of the way. He reached into his backpack and pulled out what looked like a tube. A stream of dark liquid shot from it, splashing three of the four letters with thick black goo. He tore off his ski mask and spun to face the street, a dark mane of hair cascading onto his shoulders. He held the tube high over his head, and the crowd roared its approval. A simultaneous roar came from inside the BigSky building. David ran to the war room and found the team members with their faces pressed against the glass.

33

BUILD-OUT

Sunday, January 2. David rose early. He needed to keep some semblance of rhythm in his life, even if it was nothing more than his Sunday habit of scanning *The Times* over a dish of comfort food. His mother had maintained this ritual his whole life, and it was deep in his blood and bone.

With practiced ease, he sautéed some onions and red peppers and tossed in a handful of diced pastrami and merguez, along with smoked mushrooms. He stirred a tablespoon of Pommery mustard into the mixture. On the other burner he fried an egg, sunny side up, and then laid it on top of the hash. Setting his coffee next to his plate on the breakfast bar, he sat down and unfolded the paper.

The story of "The Bull Building Climber" was front page news.

A large photo taken from the street showed the crane, the platform, and the triumphant climber with long hair, holding the dark plastic tube overhead. In the background were the huge gold letterforms of the Bull logo, splattered with violent splashes of black paint.

The climber was a woman.

The symbolism couldn't be more obvious. Richard Bull was damaging the habitat, the ecosystem, the planet itself—the mother of all earthly life. The Bull Building Climber had simply made the same courageous statement that women have been making since the dawn of time. It didn't take a genius to get the message. The black stain of guilt falls squarely on rapacious men. In this case, the rapacious men had a powerful, reckless leader.

He cleared the dishes and got ready for work, his sense of purpose renewed. The forces that threatened nature and beauty cannot be allowed to succeed.

He found Sokrates waiting at the curb. As he clambered into the back seat, he could tell something was wrong. The atmosphere in the car was decidedly chilly. He tried an icebreaker.

"Hi, Sok."

"Hey, man."

"Did you see the paper this morning?"

"Yeah, I saw it." No joy in his voice.

"What's the matter?"

He took a deep breath. David waited him out. "This whole Bull thing," he finally said.

"What about it?"

"It's my mother. She has COPD. Had it for years. The thing is she's never smoked. The doctor thinks it was fumes from the coal-fired power plant in our crappy old neighborhood."

Build-out

"She okay?"

He shook his head no. "She needs a more expensive treatment. Naturally, Bullcare doesn't cover pre-existing conditions. She's out of luck."

"I'm so sorry, Sok. What can I do?"

"Nothing. It's not your fault. Just the way the world wobbles."

They arrived at BigSky headquarters to find the crane still in place, with all the letters removed except for the last *L*, which had been spared the climber's black paint. A few media trucks were still there, along with a knot of gawkers taking photos on their phones.

"Let me know what happens with your mom," said David. He squeezed Sok's arm and made his way up to the office.

The mood in the war room was bright. The talk revolved around the new website and how it might change attitudes, including, apropos of the morning news, attitudes about oil extraction in sensitive wildlife areas.

Raven, Talia, and Michael had drawn a chart of tiered offerings based on input from Cary. They were arranged as a ladder, from the lowest level of engagement at the bottom to the highest level at the top. These would tie to the revenue model:

Contributor level
Membership level
Personal concierge
Total trip insurance
Booking engine
Personalized itineraries
Dreaming level

"The bottom rung of the ladder is what we're calling *dreaming*," said Raven. "To get you thinking about your next vacation, TripBuilder will offer some of the elements of a travel magazine: articles on destinations, hotels, restaurants, activities, and so on. Users can browse, share, and print them out for free.

"The next tier up is the actual trip builder, the AI-driven itinerary-maker. This is also free. You can generate as many itineraries as you like. No limit. You can also share them with friends. This is the heart of the website.

"Let's say you decide to purchase one of your itineraries. You'll pay for everything at once—tickets, hotels, rental cars, tour guides—everything. The cost of these items will be the same as if you bought them directly from the vendors. The difference is that TripBuilder makes it easier. Each vendor will pay BigSky a small commission.

"For a modest premium, you can add insurance to your trip. This will cover your whole itinerary, not just certain parts of it."

David stopped her. "What if people just want insurance for their flights, or just their hotels?"

Raven looked at her teammate. "Tally?"

"I've put together some numbers," she said. "Since we'll control the entire trip, we can offer a much better price than all the individual policies added together. Of course, we could also offer the insurance à la carte, but the premiums will be so cheap that we think people will choose the total coverage."

David was skeptical, but offered his provisional assent.

"For a little bit more," continued Raven, "they can buy a different kind of insurance—their own twenty-four-hour concierge. This service would be available at all hours, day or night, to help solve any problem that comes up: An issue at the airport. Lost baggage. A sudden change of plans. Their concierge would be their own personal 'fixer.'"

"And the next tier?"

"Regular travelers could move up to the membership level and get these and other services at a discounted rate. For example, fast-tracking through security. Lounge passes with partnering airlines. Hotel discounts. So on and so forth."

"What about the next level? The 'contributors'?" said Shigeru, pointing to the top tier.

"These are the most engaged customers, our thought leaders. They'll contribute articles, lead tour groups, manage forums, speak at conferences. We can't grow the brand without growing our core contributors."

"Makes sense. What's next?" said David.

"We're working out pricing and costs so we can finalize our revenue model. Keep in mind," cautioned Raven, "these would need to be tested and refined."

David and Shigeru headed to the other side of the room. Yasemin and the Thompson Twins were taping a series of home-page printouts to the whiteboard. David's eyes danced when he took in the dramatic photos and crisp layouts. He could see Yasemin's hand in them.

"Yaz," he said, "can you walk us through the various concepts?"

"They're pretty self-explanatory," she said. "Cary found some insights on what works and doesn't work for this type of site. The main thing we tried to do is reduce cognitive overhead—people thinking too much. Users hate not knowing where they are in a site. They need to feel they're in control. That means removing any clutter, disorganization, hard-to-read typography, gratuitous music, flashing images, and distracting videos in the periphery of their vision."

Aduwa chimed in. "They also dislike baffling navigation schemes and vaguely titled links. They get impatient with slow loading times. They hate losing data when they make a mistake. So we tried to build in forgiveness."

"Forgiveness?" said David.

"Sort of like a safety net. It's based on the principle that most user mistakes are really design flaws. We always try to build in guardrails so people can't drive off the road."

"The other thing that stops adoption," said Braley, "is a sense of being manipulated. If users can't understand how you're making money, they start looking for hidden agendas. This can usually be mitigated with clear design and copywriting. We could even include a brief statement about our profit model right here," he said, indicating the "About" link.

Aduwa pointed to the left of the link. "And here's where the new name goes." She looked over David's shoulder. "How's that coming, Cary?"

David turned to see Cary standing behind him. She had a yellow pencil in her mouth and a fraying topknot in her hair. He felt the familiar lightning race down his spine.

She smiled and laid six logos on the table. Each was rendered in a different typeface:

TrekPlanner	*GoThere*
Lewis & Smart	**Bucketeer**
Voyageur	Safari

"We used TripBuilder as a starting place. Descriptive names like TripBuilder are generic—which means they're the hardest to protect legally. So we tried to be a little more imaginative."

"Can you give us your thinking?" said David.

"Well, before I start, you have to understand that we're not happy with any of these. This is first-pasture thinking."

"First what?" said David.

Build-out

"First-pasture thinking. If you let horses into a pasture to eat the grass, some will stop just inside the gate where the grass is easiest to get to. The problem is, it's been trampled by previous herds. The pickier horses go up to the next pasture, where the grass is fresher. The pickiest horses of all go to the top, where the grass is pristine and delicious—that's third-pasture thinking."

"Are you a picky horse?" said David with a mischievous smile.

"A *verrry* picky horse," she said.

"Go on," said Shigeru, with a sidelong glance at David.

"TrekPlanner is one step less generic—meaning more protectable—than TripBuilder. What's good about it is this." She underlined *Trek*. "Toothy word, that. Dayna says it has good *mouthfeel*."

"Next, Lewis and Smart is a play on Lewis and Clark, of Oregon Trail fame. It sounds like a classic British travel agency. So the typography is classic, even stuffy—but in a good way." She circled the ampersand.

"*Voyageur* is French for traveler. In France the name would be generic, but everywhere else it would seem exotic. But we have *un petit problème*. The spelling is also exotic. Not good." She slashed a diagonal line through the name.

"GoThere." She scribbled over the top of it. "Too boring." She moved to the next logo.

"Bucketeer is a pretty good name for a site that lets you check off your bucket list. But it's a bit, I don't know…"

"Comical?" offered Shigeru.

"Flip," she said. "People are spending thousands on their dream vacations. We probably shouldn't reduce their dreams to a punchline."

David and Shigeru agreed.

"Then there's Safari. The concept of a safari fits well with our general theme of nature travel. But the problem is, it too is generic. We'd have to combine it with another word, something like Big-Safari or GoSafari."

David frowned.

He and Shigeru went back and re-examined the work of all three teams, placing colored dots on the ideas they found most promising. When they finished, Shigeru called the group together to direct its next moves.

"Great work, everyone. Some strong themes emerged from the first round of the scramble. We were intrigued by the dreaming level of the tiered-engagement chart. Dreaming is free, and takes relatively little effort for users. It's also the first step toward desire. Let's see if we can pump that up."

"In the website work, the most effective approaches—large, seductive photos and clear typographic treatments—seem to do just that. There are also arrows, like signposts, that lead you further into the site, and little maps and distance scales, classic symbols of travel and navigation.

"Of the six naming directions, Safari seems to be the closest to what we want. Let's see if we can alter it somehow, or else capture the same feeling in a different name."

David noticed Raven shaking her head slowly, as if she couldn't believe her senses.

"Raven, what's wrong?"

"Is this how it's done?" she said.

"How is what done?"

"Innovation."

They all laughed. They were picking up speed, and the exhilaration was thrilling.

34

BULLETPROOFING

Monday, January 3. David reached for his phone on the nightstand. The clock read *6:30 a.m.* He tapped the button for the *Journal* and scrolled through the business section. To his dismay, the headline for the article was worse than he'd expected. Another hit job.

BigSky Weighs Change at Top

By NATHAN TENEBRI

NEW YORK, NY—In a looming showdown that reflected intense pressures on the travel industry, BigSky, Inc. is weighing the replacement of its chief executive, David Stone. Mr. Stone has led the company for a year, but has been unable to halt the downward slide of its stock price.

Last week Mr. Stone terminated the company's chief of operations, Stephen J. Cochran, for what the company euphemistically called "differences on strategic direction." According to sources, Mr. Cochran had been a stellar performer for the previous six years.

It was recently revealed that BigSky's board of directors had given Mr. Stone until January 5 to present a viable turnaround plan. The outcome of the meeting will determine whether he stays in the position or is asked to step down.

In an interview yesterday, Mr. Stone acknowledged that the company was facing severe problems, and that his executive team was planning a new business that could lead BigSky back to profitability. When asked about the plan, he said only, "We intend to transform the travel industry." He declined to support his assertion with concrete details. BigSky's annual meeting is slated for January 19. Any replacement for Mr. Stone would be announced at that time.

David threw off the bed covers. How did they know about the presentation? Who leaked? It could have been Steve, but it also could have been anyone else on the board, even Andy. But why? David's little boast of transforming the travel industry now looked like the ravings of a condemned man.

He showered and quickly dressed. An urgent text to Sokrates went unanswered. He took the next available Uber, emailing Raven and Michael on the way. Andy would have to wait for an explanation until he powwowed with his team.

"Unintended consequences," said Raven. "I'm really sorry. It looks like my advice backfired."

"What can we do?" said David.

"Realistically," said Michael, "I think we're already doing it. The only credible rebuttal to an article like that is to win."

David had to agree. He was just about to email Andy when he

received a text: *Just keep your eye on the ball.* —A.

The taskforce teams were busy working through further iterations. The website was coming along well. The layouts showed a pleasing combination of clean graphics and rich information, which the Twins referred to as "simplexity." They'd managed to capture the feeling of a safari without the slightest hint of corniness. There were no zebra stripes, jungle motifs, bamboo lettering styles, or hand-drawn maps. The breathtaking magnificence of nature came across in the photos, colors, and clean typography.

David met with Talia, Michael, and Raven, who were digging into revenue models and forecasting methods. Talia had pulled up a formula for estimating the "network effect" that comes from being first in a social marketplace. It was drawn from Metcalfe's law, an axiom stating that the value of a network grows with the square of its users.

"Think about Amazon," Talia explained. "The more customers they get, the more reviews they get. The more reviews they get, the better their recommendations. The better their recommendations, the more value they add to customers. The network effect creates an upward spiral that eventually makes competition irrelevant."

"Sounds like an unfair advantage," said Michael.

"It is," said Talia, eyes gleaming. "Imagine our back-end software becoming the de facto operating system for travel."

David wrote *network effect* and *operating system* in his notebook and moved on to talk with the trademark team.

Dayna said she hadn't found time to finish the naming. She was busy writing copy for the home page and second-level pages for the twins. Bel had turned her attention to an idea she had for a collateral piece. David asked if they could set their projects aside and start building the presentation. He recruited Shigeru. The four of them moved to a corner of the war room and started making a list of the slides he would need.

"My advice is to keep the presentation simple," said Bel, "like the website. There's no reason to bombard the board members with bullet points." Dayna and Shigeru concurred—clarity, strength, and confidence are preferable to fast-talking salesmanship and reams of data. They began building a framework for the main ideas David would need to address. They expanded the original slide deck to include six topic areas:

> *The Situation*
> *The Opportunity*
> *The Tribe*
> *The Experience*
> *The Plan*
> *The Projections*

"Bel," said David, "let's use these as subhead slides. You can decide whether they need to be illustrated or not. Shig, you and Dayna work together writing supporting slides for each of these topics, based on the work we've done so far. No more than five slides for each topic, one point per slide. Okay?"

"I suppose one way to bulletproof a presentation," said Shigeru, smiling, "is to remove all the bullets."

"Ta-*dup*," said Dayna, imitating a snare drum.

David smiled. "We also need a main title. I'm putting you in charge, Dayna."

"Yes sir!" She saluted stiffly, like a sailor on the HMS *Pinafore*.

It looked like another late night. Talia called Capizzi and ordered another round of pies.

After dinner, David and Shigeru looked over the latest output from the website team, comparing the features with the experience

Bulletproofing

chart. Their progress was solid. The twins promised a working demo by morning.

Cary and Dayna, regrettably, hadn't been able to get to the naming work. Cary was busy testing home-page layouts with users, and Dayna was writing copy for the presentation.

David met with Raven to compare notes. He was surprised to find that she didn't seem tired after such a long day. On the contrary, she seemed energized.

"David, I have to say, this project has been a real eye-opener. I've never felt so, so—*alive*—as I have in the last few weeks. I've never been particularly creative, or imaginative, or innovative. But I *love* this idea. It has such incredible potential. Thank you for including me. I've learned so, so much."

David was taken aback by this sudden show of appreciation. He'd always seen Raven as a dutiful soldier, a stoic field general, not an effusive or demonstrative colleague. Had he misjudged her?

"Raven," he said, "I really respect your practicality. Tell me how you'd develop this business." The two leaders talked for nearly three hours, probably longer than they'd talked the whole previous year.

It was now 11:00. He returned to the war room to check on the others. Everyone had gone except for Cary, who had taken a break from vetting Dayna's latest batch of names.

"Any luck?"

"I'm beat," she said, shutting her laptop. "My brain has ceased all functioning. The hamsters have jumped off the wheel. I'll start again tomorrow when I'm fresh."

"Don't lose sleep over it," said David. "Remember, we're not building a finished brand. It's just a prototype. If the board buys into it, we'll have time to refine the name."

Cary brightened at this.

"Listen, I've got a car coming in five minutes," said David.

"Drop you off at your hotel?"

Sokrates, upon seeing David with a woman, jumped out of the car and opened the door. He looked at David quizzically, as if to say, "Who is this vision of loveliness?"

"Cary, meet Sokrates," he said, "my friend and personal Uber driver. Don't tell anyone. He'll be barred or arrested or whatever they do to maverick drivers."

"Call me Sok," he said with a courtly bow. Then to David, "Sorry, I was busy this morning."

They scooted into the back seat and Sokrates closed the door. As they drove, David asked Cary how she thought it was going.

"Good, overall." She was about to say something else, when she glanced nervously at Sokrates and paused.

David reached forward and pushed the privacy button. The window slid up silently.

"Is it soundproof?" she said.

David nodded.

"Raven told me something yesterday I thought you should know."

"What?"

"The reason Steve isn't happy. His wife left him."

"When?"

"About two months ago. Apparently, he was fooling around with a woman here in the city. His wife found a receipt in his coat pocket. Dinner for two at a restaurant he said he'd never heard of."

David shook his head. "I've met his wife. She's lovely. What was he thinking?"

"That's not all. Raven overheard him on the phone talking with someone at IBM. They were discussing the feasibility of using AI to power a travel website."

David stiffened. "Steve? He hated the idea. I had to fire him over it."

Cary shrugged. "Raven thought it was best to let sleeping dogs lie. I convinced her that *this* dog could wake up and bite us."

"Why are you telling me this?"

"Because I think you're a jerk and deserve to fail," she said, jabbing his chest. "Why do you think I'm telling you?"

David had a sudden urge to brush back a strand of her straw-like hair.

"Give me your phone," she said. He handed it over. She punched in her phone number and gave it back. "In case you need anything."

As they pulled up to the hotel, David lowered the privacy window and wished her goodnight. She thanked them both and walked toward the revolving doors. David wondered why he'd never noticed her figure before.

35

WIND-UP

Tuesday, January 4. The apartment was cold that morning. David turned the shower knob to *H* and waited for the water to heat up. He hadn't slept well. He couldn't stop thinking about the question Sokrates had asked him on New Year's Eve: *Is there one thing you could tell the directors—anything at all—that would force them to fund the project?*

Force might be too strong a word. What about *inspire*? It had to be their choice.

The water ran down his body in warming streams. He couldn't shake the idea that the key to selling the strategy lay in the logic of network effects. Talia's point was that a fast-growing network locks in customers while locking out competitors. The world doesn't need two Amazons. It doesn't need two Googles. And it probably doesn't need two TripBuilders. Just one good one. He suddenly realized he hadn't thought this through. Their problem statement was incomplete. He shut off the water and threw on his clothes.

Sokrates was unavailable, so he called another car. On the way in, he checked the price of BSKY. The articles in the *Journal* had taken their toll. The stock was down another three points. *Keep your eye on the ball.* He checked his inbox. PR had sent him a message saying there were seventeen emails from news outlets requesting information, comments, and interviews. The *New York Times*, *Barron's*, *Strategy+Business*, *Forbes*, *Los Angeles Times*, *Chicago Tribune*, and *Miami Herald* would have to wait.

As soon as he got to the office he joined Raven, Talia, and Michael, and brought over Dayna and Shigeru.

"Remember our problem statement?" he said. "The first of the five *P*s?" Shigeru dug through his notes and read it aloud.

"Problem: The hotel industry has experienced a serious downturn—"

"No, not that part," said David. "The opportunity part."

"Opportunity cost: If we do too little or nothing at all, we'll stay on a downward path of disappearing customers, falling revenues, shrinking profits, and possibly the sale of our assets. Thousands of people could lose their jobs."

"It's missing something."

"What?" said Shigeru.

"The network effect. We've been thinking about the advantages of being first—of locking competitors out by locking customers in. Talia raised the possibility of becoming a sort of operating system for travel. But we haven't thought about the situation in reverse. Sure, we want to lock out competitors, but only from the online travel agency business. We plan to be fair to competitors by featur-

Wind-up

ing their properties alongside our own without bias. But we can't be sure that they would behave the same way. They might easily use AI to favor their own hotels."

"I'm not sure I get it," said Talia.

"I do," said Michael, his neck muscles tensing. "If we do little or nothing, one of our competitors could take the idea and lock *us* out. Not just from the online agency business, but the hotel business too. *They'd* become the operating system for travel, and we'd be paying for access. Bloody hell."

Their eyes widened as the full extent of the danger sank in.

"This is the final selling point to the board," said David. "We have to show them that a huge opportunity, if not seized, can become a threat. Talia, can you and Cary work up two forecasts? One showing the future of BigSky with TripBuilder, and another one showing what would happen if a less scrupulous competitor beat us to it?"

"Oh, this is good," said Raven. "Now you're speaking the language of the board. They're all about mitigating risk. We need to show them that doing nothing would be the most dangerous course of all."

"Exactly. In the meantime, let's run through the presentation as it stands. I need to start rehearsing for tomorrow. Raven, Michael, Talia: Can you help me with some role-playing?"

They agreed immediately.

"Great. The rest of you, take a few minutes to imagine the toughest questions the board might ask me. Focus on the viewpoints of Andy, Catherine, and Phil."

Raven, Michael, and Talia stationed themselves around the table in the formal conference room where the presentation would take place. Their notes lay spread out in front of them.

David stood behind his laptop at the opposite end of the table from the screen, clicking through slides. Dayna, Shigeru, and Bel had done a fine job writing and designing the secondary points. They were succinct, hard-hitting, authoritative. There was nothing extraneous, nothing to distract from the core proposal. The website demo wasn't quite finished. That would have to be dropped in later, along with the final slides showing the opportunity cost.

He clicked to the title slide. For now, it said *Name to come.* It was followed by the headline, "A once-in-a-lifetime opportunity for BigSky." The words floated in a field of blue above a winding trail that disappeared into the distance. He recognized the stunning landscape of Torres del Paine in Patagonia. Clouds, like white wedding rings, circled tall jagged peaks.

David clicked to the next slide, "The Situation." He ran through the problem statement, the facts of their declining revenues, his failed attempts to stem the tide. He showed how their situation mirrored that of competitors. He presented the causes with familiar images—newspaper headlines on travel bans, long security lines in airports, stranded passengers sitting on the floor, the depressing aftermath of terrorist attacks.

He moved on to "The Opportunity," describing how they could turn a bad situation to their advantage by addressing the difficulties and fears that surrounded travel.

In the section labeled "The Tribe," there were photos of happy travelers, all ages and ethnicities, enjoying vacations in beautiful, exotic locations. He explained how they intended to grow the tribe beyond the current crop of hotel customers.

He skipped over "The Experience" section, since the website demo was still unfinished.

He moved to "The Plan," a set of slides with a timeline for rollout, and cost estimates for development.

Wind-up

A "Questions" slide marked the stopping point. The role-players applauded enthusiastically. Michael was the first to raise his hand. "This is Phil. As you know, we're in the hotel business, not the website business. How do you know you can pull this off?"

"Thanks, Phil. We're confident we can tap the gig economy for a team of best-in-class consultants, then recruit a few key employees from the team. The design and build won't be easy, but neither was inventing a whole new category of hotels with Sojourner."

"David, it's Catherine," said Talia. "This seems like an extravagant project. How much would it cost to launch?"

"Catherine, the experience of other companies shows we're looking at roughly $5 million to complete the beta site.

We'll know more after we run through a few more rounds of prototypes and test the basic features with customers. We can add extra features in stages, if funding the total number becomes an issue."

"This is Andy," said Raven. "As you know, I've supported you in the past. But here I have to agree with Phil. Our biggest successes have been with hotels, not travel websites. It's fine to disrupt an industry, but why not just launch another hotel chain like Sojourner? Why a website business?"

"Good question, Andy. This brings me to the crux of our research. I've been saving this slide for last." He clicked to the slide titled "The Projections," and took them through Talia's numbers. "Finally, the chart on the left estimates the gains we could make by seizing this opportunity. The chart on the right shows the costs of letting a competitor grab it first."

Before they could challenge his assertions, Cary burst into the room. "Sorry for interrupting, guys. Reality has a nasty habit of embarrassing theory. The customer demos are showing that people don't understand the itineraries. They're too complicated, at least the way they're presented in the prototype."

"Oh, man," said David. "That's the heart of the user experience."

He ran from the room so quickly that he left the others blinking in surprise.

Talia switched up their meal tradition, substituting Thai food for the usual pizza. After all the plates and takeout cartons had been cleared, Dayna placed six more names on the table. Cary and Bel hovered nearby. Michael and Raven came over to look:

GAYA   Trailhead

Machete   HENRY

Econaut   **Trek**Builder

"Let me walk you through these," said Dayna. "Our last direction in the scramble was to capture the feeling of a safari. Not an African safari, per se, but the exciting feeling that comes with getting out into the wild.

"The first name, Gaya, is a custom spelling of Gaia, the Greek goddess. She's the mythological mother of all life. It's also the name of a fringe theory that says the planet is a single, living system.

"Machete is just what you think it is—a big blade to cut through the underbrush. Our new site cuts through the complexity of travel planning and reveals a clear path. Might be too scary for some people.

"Over here, an econaut is the earthbound version of an astronaut. This is a neologism, a made-up word, which Cary says is easier to protect.

"Next, a trailhead, as you know, is the gathering spot at the beginning of a trail. Fancy ones have little kiosks with informa-

Wind-up

tion, some maps, maybe a few signposts. Our site is a virtual trailhead, the beginning of an adventure."

"What, or who, is Henry?" asked David.

"Henry the Navigator, the Portuguese prince who led the Age of Discovery. Personal names can be great, and they're relatively rare in today's brand world.

"Finally, there's TrekBuilder. This is a variation of our placeholder name, TripBuilder, using a more rustic word for *trip*. Treks are really what we're about."

The team members looked at each other, waiting for someone to make the first comment. David spoke up.

"They're all great, Dayna. Really. I can see any of these working. Even Henry, with the right attitude. But I feel like TrekBuilder is a little, I don't know…"

"Clunky?" said Dayna. "Me too."

"How about Trekster?" volunteered Yasemin.

Braley rolled his eyes. "No offense, Yaz, but if I hear one more name that sounds like Napster I'm going to pukester. Also, Napster is famous for tanking. Why create an association like that?"

"I keep circling back to Safari," said David. "The word has a nice feeling to it."

Cary had her laptop open. "I got it," she said, staring at the screen. "*Safaar*—an obscure version of safari. Wait, wait, wait." She clacked a few more keystrokes. "It's not taken!" She blew a clump of hair from her eyes and waited for the reaction.

They looked at each other and shrugged, as if to say, "Not bad."

Dayna chimed in. "I see a couple of good things about it. First, Safaar sounds comfortable next to Sojourner. Part of a family. BigSky is the parent brand; Sojourner and Safaar are the offspring brands. The second thing is that Safaar has homophonic hints of *so far*. As in, the website will take you *so far*. Or, this is my life *so far*."

"Love it, love it, love it," said Yasemin. The others agreed there was a certain affinity between the names, with their matching initial *S*s.

Thirty minutes later, Bel came back with a prototype. She'd chosen a classic font, Garamond, as the basis for the trademark.

Safaar

She had redrawn the ascender on the lower-case *F* to harmonize with the curved strokes of the lower-case *A*s. She also modified the lowercase *R* to match. The result was reminiscent of marsh plants bending in the wind. Approval was unanimous.

"Bel, hand the file off to the twins," said David. "Let's get this thing wrapped."

It was nearly 9:00. No one was ready to leave. The twins and Yasemin were finalizing the website. The problem had been the itineraries, which were laid out in a vertical list like the driving directions on Google Maps. Cary's users had found the format confusing. The itineraries contained multiple modes of travel and often ran onto a second or third page, making it hard to see the whole trip.

Yasemin performed another of her magic tricks. She flipped the timeline sideways so it ran across the screen from point *A* to point *B*, instead of down the page from number *1* to number *2*. People don't travel down, she realized, they travel across. Once again, David had to admire the quality of Yasemin's thinking. A horizontal timeline could accommodate any number of graphic inventions, which would help set Safaar apart.

Bel and Dayna were now working on some last-minute collateral. Everyone had some excuse for not going home.

At midnight, they finally let it go. They put on their coats,

Wind-up

gloves, and woolen hats. David gathered the group together one last time in the war room. They hugged their goodbyes. The twins would be heading to Prague to work on another project. Shigeru would fly back to Silicon Valley in the morning. Cary would stay in New York for a few days of R & R. David had promised the BigSky team the rest of the week off. Only Raven demurred, saying she had more work to do.

He thanked everyone with a sincerity they normally might have found embarrassing. "I don't know what to say, guys. There's no way I can express what I'm feeling right now. This has been the most intense creative experience of my life. I'll never forget it. And I'll never forget the gift you've given me—your time, your trust, your friendship." His voice cracked.

Talia came over to hug him. They crowded around, making shushing sounds.

"Snap out of it, big boy," said Raven. "We need you fresh and strong for tomorrow. Got everything you need?"

"I think so."

"Remember," said Michael. "Keep it short and sweet." He held up a forefinger.

"Uh-oh, here it comes," said Talia.

"Brevity is the soul of wit," he said. "Shakespeare."

"Brevity is the soul of *lingerie*," Cary said. "Dorothy Parker."

David did a double take.

"Go Rainiers," she mouthed silently.

PITCH

Wednesday, January 5. The meeting wasn't until noon, but David got up at 7:00 to clear his mind and run through the slides. He scooped a cup of Early Bird granola into a bowl of Greek yogurt with chopped apples and set it next to his laptop on the kitchen bar. There was an email from Andy with a link to the *Journal*. His message: *Call me as soon as you leave. I'll meet you at the entrance.* When David clicked on the link, his heart sank.

Will BigSky's CEO Lose Control?

By NATHAN TENEBRI

NEW YORK, NY—BigSky's CEO David Stone will meet with his board of directors today to learn whether he will have a job tomorrow. The company's stock price took another hit yesterday, losing 5 percentage points over the last week. His recent firing of star performer Stephen J. Cochran, and Mr. Stone's inability to enact a turnaround, have led to speculation that he may be replaced before the annual meeting on January 19.

In a recent interview, Mr. Stone told the *Journal* he planned to "transform the travel industry." It has since been learned that his plan includes using artificial intelligence to automate travel itineraries for users. Analysts generally believe that AI technology is too costly and unreliable for such complex challenges. Investors may be expressing similar views with their devaluation of the stock.

Mr. Stone has a reputation for changing professions when faced with difficulties. His first career was as a baseball pitcher for the minor-league Tacoma Rainiers. He unexpectedly quit after intentionally hitting a batter.

If Mr. Stone resigns, or is forced to leave, it is widely thought that chairman Andrew Vineyard would step in to run the company he founded. This may not give investors much confidence, however, as Mr. Vineyard turns eighty this April and his health is believed to be fragile.

Where were they getting this stuff? He wanted to throttle Stephen J. Cochran, but there was still no proof that he was the source. Now the job of persuading the board would be doubly difficult. It felt disorienting to be stripped of his privacy and exposed to the gossip of strangers.

Sokrates was unavailable again that morning. David took a yellow cab and reached the office at 11:40. To his surprise, the entrance to the building was mobbed with reporters. Andy rushed out, smiling for the cameras and grabbing David's elbow to drag him through the gauntlet. Reporters barraged David with questions. The only one he could hear clearly was, "What are your chances for surviving this meeting?"

Once inside, Andy leaned over and said, "You're safe in here."

They walked quickly to the elevator and rode the car to the top floor. Most of the board members had already arrived, balancing cups of coffee and miniature sandwiches on their plates, talking quietly in small groups. A few offered words of encouragement, but most avoided eye contact with him. David handed a thumb drive to Danny, the AV engineer, and took the remote.

At the stroke of noon, Andy invited the members to take their seats. He sat on the left nearest the screen. Phil Stine took the seat opposite. Catherine sat near the middle, on the same side as Andy. David walked to the far end of the table and thanked everyone for coming. The lights dimmed, leaving only the sconces to illuminate the wood-paneled walls, and the LED ceiling spots to light the table in front of each guest.

"We're at an inflection point in the history of travel," he began. "The first wave of disruption came with the partial disintermediation of travel agencies by online services like Expedia and TripAdvisor. The second wave will complete the process, making traditional travel agencies obsolete through artificial intelligence. We intend to lead the second wave." He clicked to the title slide.

"Introducing Safaar."

He recapped their financial situation, listing his honest but failed attempts at a remedy. He pointed to well-documented headwinds: travel bans, xenophobia, airport and airline dysfunction. He showed how addressing these problems, not trying to work around them, was the basis of their strategy.

"Travel intelligence—information gleaned from big data," he said, "is leading to a world of personalized travel. No longer will people be forced to navigate a jungle of travel choices just to plan a trip. No longer will they have to guess at which user recommendations to trust and which to avoid. Safaar will learn their preferences and simplify their planning."

David clicked to the home page of the website. There were

Pitch

quiet gasps from the board members. Many offered nods of cautious approval. The exceptions were Catherine, who sat rigidly in her chair, and Phil, who looked bored as he regarded the city imprisoned in his snow globe.

"Let's go right to the heart of the service—Safaar's AI-powered itinerary engine. As you can see, I've already entered my personal travel preferences. Now I can start planning my trip. It's a bucket-list vacation to Machu Picchu, a lifelong dream of mine.

"I've allowed fifteen days, from December 13 through December 27. Since I'm flexible, I'll click this box. The site immediately proposes an itinerary based on availability and the experience of others with my same preferences. Another box pops up. It asks if I'd like to add a cruise up the Amazon while I'm there. This wild-card recommendation is based on the experiences of other travelers. I click *yes*, and it revises my itinerary to include a three-day river cruise in my timeline."

"What kind of cruise?" asked a board member.

"It's right here. I just touch the timeline and up comes a photo of the vessel: a deluxe touring boat with a floor-to-ceiling window in each of the private apartments. I click the arrow to see a slide show of the experience."

He touched the other sections of the timeline. Photos of each city, each hotel, and each activity appeared full screen, with the timeline floating over the top of the images. "My itinerary takes me from New York to Houston, and finally to Lima, where I stay at the Quinta Miraflores Hotel. Here's a list of museums I can visit while I'm there. Then I fly to Iquitos for my Amazon cruise. I disembark at Nauta, take the shuttle to Iquitos, and head back to Lima so I can change planes for Cuzco."

"Wow, that's complicated," said one of the members.

"A trip to Machu Picchu isn't something you want to attempt on Orbitz," said David. "From Cuzco I take the bus to Ollantaytambo, where I stay at the El Albergue for two days. Safaar tells me I need both days to adjust to the altitude.

"While I'm there I check out the ruins in the Sacred Valley. The next day I take the train to Machu Picchu Pueblo, where I stay at the Hotel Inkaterra, near the park. Safaar recommends that I visit the ruins first thing in the morning before the tour buses show up. Here's a dramatic photo of the site in the morning fog." He heard a few admiring murmurs. "Safaar suggests I also visit the park at sunset after the tourists leave. The next day I go birdwatching on the expansive hotel grounds."

"Sign me up!" blurted a board member.

"I will, Max. But, first, I want to share my itinerary with my friends on Facebook, some of whom have already been to Machu Picchu. So I click here." A cell phone chimed on the right side of the table.

"Barbara, I think you have a message. Can you read it to us?"

Surprised, she reached into her purse. "Hi Barbara," she read, "this is David. I'm going to Machu Picchu. Got any recommendations?" She laughed and passed the phone around for everyone to see.

"A click on your phone will take you to the website, where you can see my itinerary and make your own suggestions. Safaar takes full advantage of the social graph as part of our plan to grow the tribe." He clicked to the next slide.

"Here are Barbara's suggestions. I can second these by clicking on them, and my timeline redraws itself to incorporate the changes. I can make as many itineraries as I want, free, and every variation is saved as a version. Let's see, I think I'll buy this version."

He looked down the table. "Okay, Max. Here's where you sign up. All the flights, train tickets, hotels, rental cars, shuttles—every major cost for the trip is itemized here. You put in your credit card, and *voila*! Paid for. Now you can print out your travel documents.

"But let's say you're a member of Safaar Club. Danny, can you pass the packets out?" The AV engineer handed out a dozen tie-string envelopes, each with a bound booklet inside. "As a premium customer, your documents will also arrive by courier. Each booklet contains all your tickets, reservations, maps, and a customized, foldout timeline." Several of the board members had already found the accordion-fold itinerary and were stretching it out to examine the detailed graphics. He mentally praised Bel for creating such a compelling souvenir.

David could see that the board members had started to buy in. They were nodding, giggling, comparing pages in the travel pack. The only abstainers were Catherine and Phil. Catherine showed no expression at all. Phil continued to play with his snow globe, his travel pack unopened on the table.

David then shared the plan for the configuration of the team, the development schedule, and the rollout plan. He explained the engagement tiers and the pricing model. He ended with the estimated costs, and clicked to the slide that said *Questions*. They came in rapid-fire order.

"Where will the AI come from?"

"Google. We're already in talks."

"When will you reach the breakeven point?"

"About eighteen months."

"Has anyone ever done this before?"

"No. It's crucial for us to be the first."

"Is there a Plan B?"

"No. It's not pass-fail. It's test-and-iterate."

"Who's going to manage the Safaar business?"

"Raven McCanby."

A ripple of appreciation flowed through the room. Raven was a respected member of the company; her promotion to the GM spot would be well received. It was time to close the sale.

"Now, I know what you're thinking. If our plan is to start a new business, why build a website and not just another hotel chain—

something innovative, like Sojourner?"

He could see several heads bob.

"First, because we believe the eco-lodge industry will take some time to recover. Second, because the window of opportunity for Safaar is now. This is our chance. I have one more slide to show you."

He reached for the button to show Talia's financial projections —the grand finale—when Phil interrupted him.

"David, this has been interesting," he said, as if it hadn't been interesting in the least, turning the snow globe over in his hands. "To me, your idea seems like a poor fit. We've got an urgent revenue problem. Your solution would take at least two years to hit black ink. How do you propose we deal with our falling revenues in the meantime?"

It was an obvious question, and David was prepared for it. He drew a slow breath. "First of all, the key to strong performance for BigSky has always been taking the long view, not maximizing profits in the short—"

"David," interrupted Catherine, "I think what Phil is saying is that, in this case, the short-term is where the problem is."

"In my experience," continued Phil, "it's extremely difficult to develop a unique strategy. If the strategy really *is* unique, it's risky. Industries are bounded by economic models, customer expectations, well-understood competitive structures. These are almost impossible to change quickly."

"Phil," said Andy, "what are you suggesting?"

"Can I have the remote?"

David looked at Andy. Andy nodded. He handed the remote to the board member on his right. It traveled down the table to Phil, who exited out of David's presentation.

"Catherine and I have been exploring strategic alternatives. As you know, Catherine has ties with the Bull Group. One of their businesses is interested in acquiring our eco-lodge properties.

Pitch

They've just offered us an attractive premium over the estimated value." Before David could object, the board broke into loud conversation.

"Why would the properties be more valuable to the Bull Group than to us?" said one of the members.

"Because," said Phil, "they believe that BigSky's hotels don't take full advantage of their pristine locations. The Bull Group would build golf courses, helipads, and airstrips to accommodate small jets. Middle-income people have cut back on travel, but wealthy people have not." He clicked to his first slide.

"If we compare discounted cash flows, we can see a stark difference between a slow-growth business with middle-income customers and a well-funded business with high-income customers. Luxury customers would pay three-to-four times as much to stay in these locations—provided they're upgraded."

David was horrified. He looked at Andy, who seemed unperturbed.

"How soon would they be willing to deal?" said another board member.

"Almost immediately. We'd just need to finalize the price and draw up a contract. The number I showed you is just an opening offer. We can negotiate up from there."

He clicked to a pie chart showing BigSky's current cash position. The next slide showed its cash position after selling off the eco-lodges. "A quick infusion of cash would allow us to expand the airport hotels, create new hotel concepts, and, most importantly, reward the shareholders for their patience. They've been waiting a long time."

David started to feel warm. *They've* been waiting a long time. Who are "they"? Phil and Catherine? He was losing his ability to think straight. He tried, but couldn't control the fire in his brain. He found himself standing up. He strode briskly in Phil's direction, tore the remote from his hand, and grabbed the snow globe. He stalked back to his place at the end of the table. He slammed down the remote and the snow globe and leaned forward on his hands.

"We…are…*not*…going to *do* that!" he yelled in a voice not his own. "Sell off the last remaining bits of paradise on the planet? What's the matter with you? Are you even *human*?" The board members were aghast.

"A bird in the hand is worth two in the bush, isn't it, David?" said Catherine sweetly.

He was livid. "If we sell off our properties to that—that *moron*," he sputtered, "how do you think future generations will regard us? As leaders, or as traitors? Your *solution*—your fucking pie chart—is a recipe for short-term piracy and long-term *disaster*. That is *not* what BigSky is about!"

Phil slowly rose to his full height, an imposing chest of drawers that could tip forward at any moment, spilling its ugly contents over the room. His features seemed even coarser than they had at the last meeting, if that was possible.

"Son, I could buy and sell this company without even going to the bank. Don't tell me what's good for BigSky. I know what customers want. They want what I give them, and they've been happy to pay for it as long as I've been in the business. The eco-lodge category is dead. *Dead*."

David lost all cognitive control. He was a pulsing bundle of muscles, tendons, and nerves. He could feel the long-forgotten heat rising up from his legs. To his groin. To his chest. Now his face. All he could see was Phil's huge, wide forehead. It looked like the broad side of a badly constructed barn, bulging and buckling from its own weight.

Phil continued, sneering. "There's a reason the stock price keeps dropping, son. It's your total lack of experience. Your sad,

Pitch

pathetic, farmboy naïveté. We're *sick* of it."

Something snapped. With a single cobra-like move, David snatched the snow globe from the table and cocked his arm back. He felt the muscles in his shoulders tighten and flex, his fingers grip the glass dome. His torso, reaching for the maximum torque, twisted clockwise. His body was in total control now, his years of training the only determinant of what would happen next.

As his arm flashed forward, he wrenched his eyes from Phil's face. The globe flew fast and hard over the center of the table, tumbling end over end, a glittering streak of light. In his peripheral vision he could see board members recoiling, some with their arms over their faces.

The snow globe struck the center of the pie chart with the force of a cannon, smashing the oversized display into a spiderweb of sizzling circuits. Thousands of pieces of glass and tiny droplets of glycerin rained down on the board members. Some instinctively ducked. Others ran toward the doors. David stood there, feet apart, arm hanging down, his anger spent in a single, mindless action.

He was finished. He'd done the one thing he had sworn never to do again. Everything he'd been working for, all the sacrifices he'd made, vanished in a moment of runaway emotion. When the room was clear of board members, he looked helplessly at Andy.

"David," said Andy, his voice devoid of emotion. "Go home. Get some rest. Meet me here tomorrow at 11:00."

David slapped the remote off the table. He was so angry that he didn't dare speak. He stalked out of the room, and for the first time since starting at BigSky, he walked the whole way home.

David slept fitfully until four o'clock in the afternoon. He roused himself, took a shower, tried to come to grips with what he'd done.

He went down to the kitchen, poured himself a glass of Lagavulin, and dropped two ice cubes into it. His head was hot and throbbing.

What had happened? How did he get here? He thought back to the beginning of the strategy project. Five weeks was not enough time. Still, they had worked well together once they'd gotten their sea legs. If they had already known how to use the agile strategy process, they could have knocked it out in three weeks. The problem wasn't the timing—it was the leaks. The news articles had poisoned the minds of the board members, making them susceptible to a quick fix. Who was the leaker? Steve?

He thought back to the last *Journal* article. The reporter mentioned artificial intelligence. Steve certainly could have leaked that piece of information, since he knew about it from the beginning. But the timing was odd. Why treat it like a scoop?

A dark realization swept over him. The timing. That article had appeared only two days after he and Sokrates had dropped Cary at her hotel. She'd mentioned Steve's call with IBM to discuss AI services. The privacy window was up, but had their conversation truly been private? He put the thought out of his head. Sokrates was a friend. Probably his best friend.

He took another sip of whisky and rubbed his head. He thought back to the earlier article on Monday, the one that gave the date for his pitch to the board. He had told Sokrates about it three days earlier, the morning of New Year's Eve. Another coincidence?

What about the first article, the one that broke the news about firing Steve? That had actually been Sok's idea. Steve could have leaked all of those items to the paper himself, but the intervals between telling Sokrates and the publication of the articles were suspiciously alike. Two days, three days, two days. Just enough time to pull the articles together.

If Sokrates was clever enough to wire his car for sound, he was clever enough to wire it for recording behind the privacy window.

Pitch

He wouldn't do that, would he? Why? Who were the other regulars? Was he recording them too, or was he working for them? Was Phil Stine a regular?

He had trusted Sokrates. He had trusted him more than anyone in his position should have. He was so needy for friendship that he fell for the oldest con in the book—the "believe me, I'm on your side" con. To be a good leader, you have to be a good judge of character. Was he?

He felt sick. He didn't want to accept it. He couldn't accept it. To suspect Sokrates of playing him for a mark was to accept a world in which no one is reliable, no one can be trusted, where people are just out for themselves, and only suckers would befriend a stranger.

People don't go around betraying other people without a reason. Either they're professionals—spies or grifters—or they're caught in a situation they can't deal with. He remembered what Sokrates had told him on Sunday. His mother couldn't get the medical treatment she needed because the government had cut her coverage. He may have needed the money. Would that be enough to justify selling out a friend? It might be. Especially if your whole life had been an uphill battle, made more difficult by gangs, corrupt police, and a system that favors the rich.

How could anyone be so stupid? What did Stine call it—his "sad, pathetic, farm-boy naïveté"? A perfect description of the greenhorn Stone. All this time he thought Sokrates was a confidant. Instead, he was a confidence man. A garden-variety industrial spy. Welcome to the major leagues, he thought.

He downed the rest of his whisky, poured another. Nothing mattered now. His career as CEO was over. When the news about his stupidity finally leaked out, no company in the world would hire him. He dropped into a dark, dreamless chasm, and didn't wake up until the next morning.

37
AFTERMATH

Thursday, January 6. The bright blue sky was a jarring contrast to his altered reality. Pedestrians hurried along the sidewalks, carrying on with their busy lives, unaware that the world had ended for a certain nobody named David Stone. The crane was stationed once again in front of the Bull Building. The replacement letters were going up, this time without an audience of protesters, police, and media to mark the occasion.

This nobody, this David, had tried to kill Goliath. Instead, he had killed everything he prized—his job, his career, his relationships, his self-respect, his hopes for the future. There was nothing left but to apologize to Andy, pack up his office, and slip away to a new life somewhere far from New York. Maybe he'd go back to the Northwest, get a job in architecture, eventually start his own practice. His hard-earned reputation as a quitter was assured.

He rode the elevator to the top floor for the very last time. He found Andy sitting behind his forty-year-old desk. A stack of fresh newspapers sat on the side. David waited for the words he knew would come.

"That was some performance you gave yesterday."

"Andy, I'm so sorry. I'll start packing up—"

"What were you thinking?"

"I wasn't thinking, that was the problem. I'll be out of here in—"

"You're not fired."

"—an hour. *What?*"

"You're not fired." He motioned David to a chair. "Sit down. There are some things you need to know."

David sat with a thud.

"Phil and Catherine were completely out of line yesterday. What they tried to pull behind my back, this whole maneuver with the Bull Group, was reprehensible. I met with the rest of the board this morning and we agreed. Phil and Catherine tendered their resignations this morning on the condition that we don't sue them for breach of fiduciary duty. Sorry you had to be involved, but I couldn't make my move until they played their cards."

"You knew about it?"

"Of course. Do you really think I'd sell my life's work to the highest bidder? I got suspicious when a few members of the board, led by Stine, starting pressing for a turnaround. Don't get me wrong—we're in trouble—but not *that* much trouble. Their little plan was to scare the shareholders with false rumors so they could pressure the board into selling. How much money they stood to gain, I don't know. But it was probably substantial if their track record is any indication."

"So it was Stine who leaked to the *Journal*? How did you find out?"

"I wasn't sure, so I slipped a tracer into the conversation. I told him privately that my health was 'fragile.' I said, 'Whatever you do, don't repeat this information to anyone.' Yesterday, the word *fragile* popped up in the article."

"Is it true?"

"No. I'm as strong as an ox. But I needed to give him something that no one else could know, not even my doctor. In a way, my health *is* fragile." He chuckled. "At eighty, let's face it, your grip on life is tenuous."

David began to appreciate why Andy was still in control of his company. Wily didn't begin to cover it.

"Where did he get the other information, the story about my baseball scandal?"

"He could have looked that up. But he didn't have to. He got it from Steve, who was helping them every step of the way. Catherine had introduced Steve to the Bull Group months ago. They needed someone to run the company they were planning to buy. Who better than the person who'd been running it already? Steve sold his soul to become CEO."

"But how could he take the job when he was signed to a non-compete?"

"He wouldn't have to start the job until after the term of the agreement. Remodeling the lodges would take at least a year. In the meantime, he could live off his severance and work with the Bull Group in an unofficial capacity."

David threw himself back in his chair. "Those meetings. They explain the gaps in his schedule. He was busy betraying us."

Andy nodded.

"And now he'll get nothing." David shook his head. He suddenly thought about Sokrates.

"Andy, I made a good friend five weeks ago. His name is Dmitri Sokouris. His understanding of business is remarkable. I know it was rash, but I started to rely on his advice. Whenever I needed him, he was there, never expecting anything in return. I believed in his goodwill with all my heart."

Andy waited.

"Yesterday, after my meltdown at the presentation, I jumped to the conclusion that he was the one leaking the information. Two and two were adding up to five. I'd trusted him with sensitive information, and he'd betrayed me. That's what I thought. I'm not sure what I'm more ashamed of—sharing sensitive information or the fact that I doubted a good friend."

"David, that's another thing you need to know. You can trust Sokrates."

David was stunned. "You know him?"

Andy smiled with his eyes. "I was his first regular. We go back a long way. When he was a teen, he got into trouble with the police. His mother was one of my best employees and came to me for help. I arranged for a lawyer and got them out of their gang-infested neighborhood.

"It was always one thing or another with Dmitri, but he was a good kid. Years later, I loaned him the money to buy a Prius. He drives me around, and I pay for his school tuition. Last week I asked him to do me a favor—to follow Steve. That's how I knew Steve was meeting with Catherine and the Bull Group."

"Did you ask him to keep tabs on me, too?"

"You mean spy on you? Hardly. Dimitri would never do that. And I'd never ask him to. Let's just say I mentioned you to him. I'm glad you two hit it off."

David thought back to the morning when Sokrates had jumped out of the car to offer encouragement to a homeless kid. "I owe" is what he'd said. "So we're what—co-protegés?"

"Something like that. Listen, David. When I hired you, I was looking for someone to continue my legacy. Not just continue it—extend it, advance it, take it in new directions. My life hasn't been just running hotels. It's been helping people find themselves, find their place in the world. I want them to gain respect for themselves, for each other, this endangered planet—this magical place. There's only one Everglades, one Yellowstone, one Grand Canyon. I had to make sure you were up to the job."

David stared at his hands.

"I knew you had talent. There was never a doubt about that." He leaned forward, his voice growing serious. "The human race is entering a dangerous phase. I realize you're only one person, David. I'm only one person. But one person with an idea can make a big difference. Before yesterday I wasn't sure you had the passion, the sheer God-given chutzpah it takes to fight such entrenched enemies. Your performance yesterday erased any doubt."

David's head was spinning. "You agree with our strategy?"

"Look, the work you did with your team is stunning. Incredible.

Superhuman. I'm really proud of you. We all are—with two unfortunate exceptions. Everyone wants to know how you got it done."

David looked sheepish. "We had no choice. There wasn't much time. We tried something called *agile strategy*."

"What's that?"

"A set of tools to help strategy teams to work faster and better. It made a huge difference."

"Well, you're going to need more tools like that. It's not going to get much easier."

"I'm not fired?"

"Not fired. Funded."

David sat frozen with a goofy grin on his face.

"What are you waiting for? Get out of here. You've got a website to build."

David stood up and lunged at Andy. He hugged him with more force than anyone should use on an eighty-year-old man. It took all of his effort to hold back his tears. He suddenly realized he was no longer "Stone by name, stone by nature." He was fully human, fully alive for the first time in years. He thanked Andy effusively and spun around to go.

"One more thing about yesterday," said Andy, the smallest hint of a smile playing on his face. "Don't ever do that again. Someone might get hurt."

David sent a quick text and raced to the elevator, his feet barely touching the floor. He reached the lobby, passed through the doors, and walked into the bright light to look for Sokrates.

The Prius was already waiting at the curb. In the back seat was a woman with blonde hair and a single red barrette.

AGILE STRATEGY

A GUIDE TO AGILE STRATEGY

I hope my story showed you how a more collaborative, all-at-once planning process beats the traditional linear model. In the following guide, I'll recap the core elements of the process itself. Let's begin by looking at the older traditional model:

 1. *Assess your current position*
 2. *Research the market for threats and opportunities*
 3. *Envision a range of scenarios*
 4. *Get agreement on a direction*
 5. *Establish a coherent vision*
 6. *Identify strategic goals*
 7. *Translate the goals into tactics*
 8. *Arrange for funding*

It's a long list of sequential steps, each step building on the previous one.

But what if you were to approach the steps simultaneously instead of sequentially? Wouldn't that speed up the process?

It would and it does. It's called *agile strategy,* an approach we've honed at our own consulting firm to work more quickly with clients. By adopting a more collaborative approach to strategy, and working simultaneously, agile teams can complete a framework for a new business or brand in fewer than three weeks. Three weeks versus three to six months.

But there's another benefit to agile strategy—the results are often more faithful to the original intent. Why? Because the various tasks are able to influence each other on the fly. The work is kept in a liquid state for as long as possible.

With the older sequential process, each step is "sealed" before the next step can be built. So, if a user-experience designer happens to discover a key idea in step seven, she'll be unable to influence the overall vision because that step has already been sealed. As a result, the sequential process can resemble a game of Telephone, in which each step draws the strategy further from its original intent and closer to a generic plan.

The agile process Cultura uses with BigSky is similar to the process we use at my own firm. We apply the five principles of *design thinking* (the five *P*s) to the five questions of *strategy* (the five *Q*s).

$$5Q \times 5P = AGILE\ STRATEGY$$

The *P*s and *Q*s are not set in stone. They're flexible, adaptable, and customizable. We use them as a starting place to address some of our toughest strategic challenges.

In this section, I'll share the basic principles of agile strategy. I'll also recommend other books and resources to help you advance from an agile-strategy novice to expert as quickly as possible.

What is design thinking?

Design thinking is the process of using prototypes to work through creative challenges. You might define it as *thinking by making*. The easiest way to understand this approach is to contrast it with traditional business thinking. Traditional thinking has two main steps: knowing and doing. You know something—because you've read about it, tried it successfully, or consider it a best practice—and then you do something. You act on it.

Design thinking has *three* steps: knowing, *making*, and doing. The middle step of making—prototyping and testing new ideas—not only challenges what you think you know, but changes what you do. It puts surprising options on the table that you hadn't known existed. Without this middle step, you're more likely to go with a safe, tried-and-true solution. While safe solutions have their place, they're inadequate if your goal is to innovate.

The five Ps of design thinking

The five *P*s are a set of principles for imagining and developing new ideas. They're specifically designed to force your mind beyond the obvious. In *Scramble,* Cary refers to "third-pasture thinking." This is the concept of going beyond the obvious to find the freshest ideas. When horses are turned out in a field to eat, the pickiest ones don't settle for the trampled grass in the lowest pasture. They climb higher, up to the second pasture, or even to the third, where the grass is truly fresh.

The five *P*s are *problemizing, pinballing, probing, protyping,* and *proofing.* Together they provide a framework for finding third-pasture ideas.

1. Problemizing

Problemizing isn't about solving problems, but about *framing* them. Never accept a problem at face value. Instead, try to find out what the real problem is—the problem behind the problem—by asking a few questions:

Agile Strategy

- *Is this the right problem to solve?*
- *Is it worthy of our best efforts?*
- *What other problems could we solve that would bring more value to our company or our customers?*

Problemizing can be divided into three steps:

1) State the problem
2) List the benefits of solving it
3) Describe the opportunity cost of ignoring it

Here's an example of how a company might problemize a situation:

PROBLEM STATEMENT #1
Our biggest competitor is stealing our customers. This has caused us to lower our prices, which in turn has forced us to lower the quality of our service. Eroding service is making it easier for our competitor to steal our customers.

SOLUTION BENEFIT
The right strategy could allow us to hold onto our customers, keep our prices intact, and deprive our competitor of market share.

OPPORTUNITY COST
If we do nothing, we'll continue on a downward spiral of lowered prices, slipping service, and vanishing customers, until our business is no longer viable.

While in problemizing mode, resist the urge to jump in with a solution. Make sure you're solving the right problem by framing it in different ways. For example, here's another way you might problemize the same situation:

PROBLEM STATEMENT #2
Our key product is no longer relevant. Its underlying technology is getting old, which has allowed one of our competitors to enter the market with a better, cheaper solution. Our first reaction was to lower the price, which put us in a downward spiral.

SOLUTION BENEFIT
By updating our product with a more advanced one, we can regain our market dominance and keep our profit margins high.

OPPORTUNITY COST
If we do nothing, the downward spiral will continue as we lower our prices, cut service quality, and watch our market share and profit margins deteriorate.

Both of these characterizations could be valid. The first one is focused on competitors, while the second one is focused on the product. How you frame the problem determines how you solve it, so it pays to get it right.

2. Pinballing

The same way a pinball bounces off obstacles and other pinballs, ideas can bounce off obstacles and other ideas. Now that you understand the problem, how many courses of action can you imagine? Our firm uses a wide range of techniques to trigger new ideas, but these are my top three:

THINK IN METAPHORS
A metaphor is a way of making a comparison between two unre-

lated things. "All the world is a stage," for example. The world is not really a stage, but it's *like* a stage in some respects. If your challenge is to invent a brand name for a store that sells footwear to active girls, for example, you could call it Active Footwear. Or you could think in metaphors and move beyond the first pasture. For example, maybe active footwear for girls is like a bouncy pop song from the Sixties—wait! What if you called it Shoebop?

ARRANGE BLIND DATES

It's possible to trigger new ideas by combining two existing ideas that haven't previously been introduced to one another. What do you get when you cross a computer store with a museum? An online shoe store with charity? A Broadway show with a circus? You might get successful business models like the Apple stores, TOMS shoes, or Cirque du Soleil. Of course, you might also get the business equivalent of kitsch, as Clairol did when it crossed hair care and yogurt and got Touch of Yogurt Shampoo, or as Omni did when it crossed a TV hit with a carbonated drink and got a beverage called Tru Blood. Don't fall in love with your first idea. Novelty and innovation are two different things.

REVERSE THE ASSUMPTIONS

Reversing an assumption can release conceptual energy. Let's say you're trying to invent a new business model for retail banking. Start by listing all the assumptions you can think of about retail banks:

- *Retail banks have spacious downtown and suburban locations*
- *They have traditional-looking interiors, with wood paneling, desks, and teller windows*

- *They have a window with a sign that lists behavioral rules, such as No bare feet, No food, and No pets*
- *Customers wait in line for the next available teller*
- *When customers open accounts, they sign multipage agreements they can't understand*
- *To apply for a loan, customers must make an appointment with a loan officer*
- *Tellers and loan officers try to upsell customers on additional financial services*
- *Banks compete for customers by lowering interest rates and downplaying fees*

Now, reverse these assumptions:

- *Our new bank has a small footprint that can fit into any retail space*
- *It has polished concrete floors, café tables, and no teller windows*
- *A sign on the window says No shoes required, Bring your pets, and Join us for a snack*
- *A representative greets customers at the door and offers them beverages*
- *When customers open an account, they sign a one-page agreement written in plain language*
- *Customers can quickly apply for a loan on their phones or ask a representative to walk them through the process on the spot*
- *Bank representatives are always looking for ways to simplify their customers' lives*
- *Our bank competes for customers by improving their lives, not by lowering interest rates*

This is pretty much how Airbank, a company in the Czech Republic, built a successful new model for retail banking.

Reversing the assumptions—and other pinballing techniques—can work equally well for starting a business, building a brand, or designing a new product or service. The goal is to put options on the table that weren't there before.

3. Probing

With new ideas in hand, you and your team can begin mining for possibilities. An excellent approach to shaping new concepts can be found in Edward de Bono's seminal book, *Six Thinking Hats*. It's based on the idea of *parallel thinking*—a technique in which the members of a brainstorming group think in the same direction at the same time. You take an idea from the pinballing stage and view it through six symbolic "hats": the white hat for information; the red hat for emotion; the black hat for caution; the yellow hat for positivity; and the green hat for creativity. The blue hat is reserved for the facilitator, who determines which hat the group wears at any given time.

When wearing the white hat, members of the group offer helpful information—marketing data, customer insights, competitive assessments, sales patterns—without suggesting any ideas or solutions.

When they wear the red hat, they're asked to evaluate an idea according to the emotions they're feeling. They may report feeling excited, nervous, cynical, intrigued, doubtful, happy, disgusted, encouraged, and so on, as long as they describe an emotion and not a judgment. As members of the team call out the emotions, the leader lists them on a large sheet of paper or a whiteboard. You'll find that people make better decisions when they confront their emotions at the start of a brainstorming session rather than cloaking them in rational-sounding arguments later.

The yellow hat is for positivity. It gives people the chance to explore the kinds of outcomes they'd like to see. It's the hat of creative wishing.

The black hat is the hat of caution and disagreement. It provides an opportunity to raise critical questions: What's wrong with this idea? How is it likely to fail? What are the possible repercussions? Black-hatting comes naturally to most of us, since we're hardwired to weigh danger more heavily than opportunity. The black hat is the hat of the naysayer, the devil's advocate. The leader can usually fill up several large sheets of paper with negative comments. The more the better. Get them out in the open. No fixes or workarounds are allowed while wearing the black hat.

Finally, the green hat is the hat of creativity. When the group wears green, only fresh, positive ideas are allowed. The goal is to transform black-hat fears into green-hat solutions.

The six-hats approach can also be used to drill down into specific features. If a new business idea includes, say, a lifetime guarantee, the group can apply the same rigor to vetting and shaping that specific feature.

4. Prototyping

Prototyping is the magic that makes design thinking more powerful than traditional thinking. It adds the making step between knowing and doing. It's the difference between *deciding* the future with off-the-shelf practices, and *designing* the future by working from first principles.

A prototype is simply a rough approximation of an idea, product, service, or process—whatever it is you're inventing. It can be a sketch, a mockup, a model, a story, or a bit of role-playing. The goal is to keep it simple, throw it together fast, and learn from the results. You then apply what you've learned to the next prototype, and so forth, round after round.

The responsibility for prototyping often lies with designers, writers, and financial modelers who use their years of training to work quickly and intuitively. Yet nearly everyone can make a sketch, tape a few objects together, or fold a piece of cardboard to approximate a product. To see how simple sketches can work wonders, take a look at Dan Roam's book *The Back of the Napkin*. It's remarkable what happens when abstract ideas are made visible.

Prototypes are essential for testing and learning. With a prototype, you can try out your ideas on prospective customers. You can see what's working, what's not working, and where to make improvements. You can use prototypes to get feedback from colleagues, bosses, or clients.

5. Proofing

Assumption is the enemy of strategic thinking. We all make assumptions about the way the world works, but assumptions can blind us to possibilities—and even reality itself. As Cary says in the story, "Reality has a nasty habit of embarrassing theory." Proofing is the fastest way to make sure your assumptions are grounded in reality.

To get the most out of proofing, test two or more prototypes against each other. When you test one at a time, you put your respondent in the position of a thumbs-up or thumbs-down assessment. With two or more prototypes, you can have a richer discussion about the relative merits of each. This is especially true when presenting your idea to your own company. Never put yourself in the position of getting a "yes" or "no" answer. Always use your prototypes as part of an ongoing conversation.

A question I often get at keynotes and workshops goes like this: "My ideas are great. But how do I get my bosses (or colleagues or teammates) to buy into them?" There are two assumptions built in to this question.

The first assumption is that ideas have to be sold like finished products. This assumes an active seller and a passive buyer. In reality, most innovative ideas aren't *bought* by bosses but *joined* by believers. When colleagues see the value of a new idea, they open up to it. They begin to see how it might benefit their company or their society at large.

The second assumption, or perhaps assertion, is that your ideas are good. Maybe they are. But from an outsider's perspective, who says? How do they know? Using which yardstick? Good for what? If you leave these questions unanswered, it should be no surprise that your ideas initially meet with resistance.

Wait, you say: "Shouldn't the value of a good idea obvious to everyone?" Well, no. You have to remember that you, the innovator, have a head start on the others. You've been working on the idea for days, weeks, even months. Not only that, you may have skills that your colleagues don't have—skills that let you envision success based on past experience. You may also be deeply passionate about the project, which is not something you can expect from everyone in your group.

So, what should you do?

Make prototypes. Test them with users. Collect evidence from your tests. Prove your idea. Apply what you've learned to further prototypes. Tell stories about the project's journey. Paint a picture of success. Enlist the support of co-conspirators. Build a coalition. The most important innovations are more like mini-movements than the work of a lone genius.

There, in a nutshell, are the basics of design thinking. If you'd like to go deeper, I encourage you to read my book *Metaskills*, or its simplified cousin, *The 46 Rules of Genius*.

But how do you get from design thinking to a workable strategy for your brand or business? By applying the five principles of design thinking to the following five questions.

The five Qs of strategy

There was a time when business strategy and brand strategy were on two different levels. Business strategy was developed at the top of the company, while brand strategy—if it existed at all—was developed at the marketing level. This is no longer true. Business strategy and brand strategy are two intertwining strands of the same DNA. The business strand represents the internal company (how you operate), and the brand strand represents the external company (how customers see you). In today's customer-centric marketplace, any company that doesn't view its customers as integral to its existence is likely to become irrelevant.

In *Scramble*, David's initial strategy efforts get lost in a confusing swirl of big-picture ideas, best-practice tactics, analytical tools, and messaging components. He needs the help of an outside firm to catalyze his thinking. He calls in Cultura. They bring structure and clarity to the strategy process, along with specialized expertise and cross-industry experience.

You can use the same process for modeling a business or framing a brand. The five Qs of strategy address the critical questions of purpose, customer, category, positioning, and culture.

1. What is our purpose?

This is the starting place for any strategy. Without a clearly defined purpose, there's no compelling reason to engage in any particular business. Leaders are more likely to bail in the face of strong headwinds. Employees will start to quit months before they actually leave. A rich, satisfying purpose makes this less likely to happen: it brings energy and motivation to everyone involved, including customers. Articulating your purpose starts by asking specific questions:

- *Why are we in business beyond making money?*
- *How do we want the world to change because of what we do?*
- *What are we passionate about?*
- *Where do our core competencies lie?*
- *How strong is the need for our products?*
- *Is this a worthy challenge?*
- *Is the challenge broad enough to encompass everything we'll want to do in the future?*

Once you articulate your purpose, you can begin draw strength from it. Build a culture around it. Develop a concrete mission, a clear vision, and measurable goals—they all flow from purpose.

In *Scramble,* Gard sketches a pyramid on the board to show how purpose fits into strategy:

At the top is *purpose.* Purpose is why you're in business beyond making money. It drives everything else, and it never changes. If a company changes its purpose, by definition it's a different company.

In the middle tier, below purpose, are two related concepts: mission and vision. Both of these answer to purpose. A mission is an ambitious goal for achieving a purpose. A vision, on the other hand, is the visualization of your mission. Microsoft, for example, declared that its mission was "to lead the personal computer revolution." But its *vision* was "a computer on every desktop and in every home." Can you *visualize* the computer on the desktop? Thus, the second tier of the pyramid gives you two views of the same goal. They're like fraternal twins. The mission and vision can last anywhere from five to twenty years.

Beneath the twin concepts of mission and vision are the various tactics, or short-term goals, that you need to accomplish them. These would be completed in, say, one to three years.

It's important to understand that your purpose can't be developed in a vacuum. You have to consider all five of the strategy questions at the same time, working back and forth to make sure they support each other.

2. Who do we serve?

You serve customers, of course. But which customers? What do they have in common? How do they communicate with each other? How likely are they to form a tribe around your brand? What are the unspoken rules of the tribe?

The biggest mistake companies make is to assume that they're in business to serve investors. This view is not only deflating for employees, but also counterproductive for the company. A company that places investors ahead of customers will eventually find it has neither.

One way to visualize how shareholders and customers fit together is with an infinity loop I call the *brand ecosystem*. It goes like this: Management nurtures employees, employees serve customers, customers attract investors, and investors support management. Investors must support management to build a sustainable company. The focus is on creating and growing your customer tribe. Everything else is secondary.

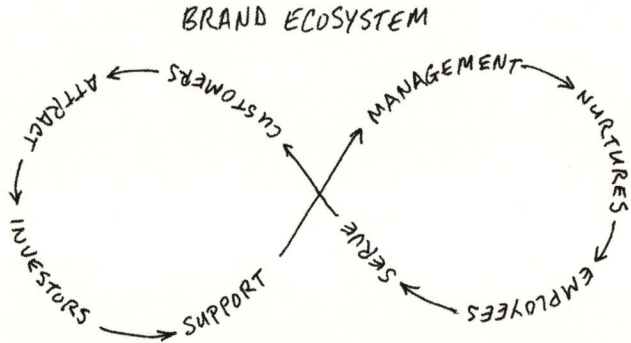

The easiest way to understand your tribe is to imagine a single, idealized customer for your product or service. At our firm, we sometimes use a *keynote speaker exercise* to help our clients think about their customers. It starts with identifying a spokesman for the brand—a well-known, well-respected individual who believes strongly in your purpose and products. If you can identify the right keynote speaker, you'll have identified your ideal customer—an advocate who can stand up for your brand and help lead the tribe.

But how can you identify your customers if you're not sure what you're selling? Once again, you have to start somewhere, anywhere, and work back and forth among the five *Q*s until they makes sense together.

Agile Strategy

3. Where should we compete?

Branding is a game of categories. The category you choose to compete in, and the products and services you sell, are key factors in your ability to win. Sometimes the category is obvious, since it serves as your starting point. But if your starting point is somewhere else, such as your overall purpose, the field broadens.

In *Scramble*, the strategy team proceeds from their company purpose instead of their existing categories. This allows them build an online travel agency instead of sticking with eco-lodges and gotels.

Whether you stay with the category you're in, or strike out in a new direction, it pays to ask tough questions like these:

- *Do we have the necessary skills to compete in this category, and with this product or service?*
- *If not, can we acquire the skills in a reasonable amount of time, and with a reasonable amount of effort?*
- *Do we already have credibility with customers in this category, or will we have to build it?*
- *Does the product or service create synergies with other products or services we're selling?*
- *Will entering the category bring us into direct competition with stronger brands?*
- *What kind of management systems will we need to support our new offering?*
- *Can we afford to do the project well?*
- *What would success look like?*

My book *Zag* is a good reference for where to compete. It also answers the next question on how to prevail over the competition.

4. How will we win?

This brings us to the most basic question: *Why will customers choose your brand over the others in the category?*

If your answer is "because our product is better," you might be kidding yourself. Customers can rarely tell which product is better. They usually base their purchasing decisions on secondary cues such as popularity, customer rankings, tribal identity, or price. Performance-based facts are less persuasive than you think.

Alternately, if your answer is "because our product is cheaper," you may be missing the point of branding. The purpose of branding is to get more people to buy more things for more years at a higher price. Trying to win by lowering the price defeats a key goal of branding—unless, of course, your brand is based on discounting. In that case, you'll need a plan to ensure that your discounts lead to sustainable profits and not to a downward spiral.

The most successful brands aren't better or cheaper. They're different. More important, they're different in ways that customers find compelling. The discipline of creating a compelling difference is commonly known as *positioning*. It's the art of finding a strategic slot in your customer's mind. You can never tell a customer what to think or which products to fall in love with. But you can produce the kind of products, messages, and behaviors that favor an advantageous position in a customer's mind.

The best test of positioning is what I call the *onlyness statement*. You can try it here. Just fill in the following blanks.

OUR BRAND IS THE *ONLY* _____ THAT _____.

In the first blank, write your category (see the third *Q* above). In the second blank, write your compelling difference. For example, Cirque du Soleil is the *only* circus with Broadway sophistication.

JetBlue is the *only* airline that offers business-class comfort for the price of coach. If you can't fill in the second blank with a clear, compelling differentiator, you probably don't have a strategy.

Even if you do, winning doesn't come from strategy alone. There are two parts to building a brand: getting the *right idea*, and getting the *idea right*. Getting it right is the more difficult of the two. Why? Because it demands the coordinated efforts of a wide range of specialists, both inside and outside the company, to create a coherent brand. Many companies are not set up to manage the rigor of branding. My book, *The Brand Gap,* describes both this problem and the solution.

5. How will we grow?

Many companies have succeeded because they took a chance and got lucky. They're the business equivalent of the baseball player who was born on third base and thinks he's hit a triple. For every one of these, there were ten who struck out and were never heard from again.

Of the companies that make it, many won't be relevant in twenty years. To succeed and grow in today's volatile marketplace, you need the ability to innovate at will—to continuously adapt to shifting circumstances.

David and his team face the same situation in *Scramble.* They find that their original eco-lodge business is no longer producing the revenues they need. Rather than try harder, they try *different.* They innovate.

For a business to be sustainable, it needs more than a good product. It needs a culture of nonstop innovation. The right kind of culture can build momentum with very small inputs, then release large amounts of energy whenever needed. This is called the *flywheel effect*. But it won't happen by simply admonishing employees to "be more innovative." It takes a steady investment in human resources, training, and reward systems. Here are five modest changes that can make a noticeable difference.

1. Elevate brand-building to the C-level. Branding is not a marketing concern. It's company concern. Appoint a chief brand officer (CBO) to manage all the interactions with the customer tribe. It's a big job, and shouldn't be run from a corner of the CMO's desk.

2. Establish an innovation center. This can be a physical space where new ideas are prototyped and tested, or a virtual space where ideas and assets are shared among employees. The main idea is to provide a home for creative collaboration.

3. Invest like a venture capitalist. A culture of innovation needs a pipeline of ideas. To vet these ideas, emulate venture capitalists by employing a stage-gate process. Start with seed money to develop a concept. Make a slightly larger investment to develop the strategy. Make a medium bet to prototype and test it. And, if the tests go well, make a large bet to launch it. Think big, spend small, build slowly.

4. Institute branded training. Companies succeed best when they differentiate from their competitors. Emphasize that difference by training employees in the unique values, methods, and processes that give your company its advantage.

5. Reward employee creativity. Send a message to the workforce that creativity is a valued skill. Rewards don't have to be monetary; they can simply offer recognition and the promise of bigger challenges. We all want the same things from our jobs: something to believe in, the ability to contribute our best, and recognition from a team we respect. You can read more about building a culture of nonstop innovation in my book *The Designful Company*.

There it is: the essence of agile strategy. For more about brand, design, and innovation, visit liquidagency.com. For more about my books, talks, and workshops, visit martyneumeier.com.

THANKS

I hope you enjoyed reading *Scramble*. I'd like to credit my friend Andrea Dorigo for urging me to attempt a business thriller in the first place, and for injecting a larger dose of verisimilitude than I could have managed on my own. His experience as a CEO and his fascination with the movie *Moneyball* inspired the main character and his backstory.

I relied heavily on other experts as well. For details of the book's imagined architectural projects, I leaned on my friend Mark Kirkhart, an award-winning architect and founder of DesignARC. He helped me conjure brilliant examples of architecture and made sure I described them with precision.

Dee Warmath, PhD, was the inspiration for Dr. Cary Blank. Dee is a font of knowledge on the subject of customer insights. In a perfect world, she (or her avatar Cary) would have been present on the strategy team from day one and not brought into the game so late.

I'd like to thank Rob Bynder for his expert advice on website design. The final scenes of the book reflect his abundant imagination and experience. For example, you may remember when Barbara Henderson's phone buzzes with a surprise text from the prototype website. That was Rob.

Many thanks to my team at Liquid, including Scott Gardner, Jim Gibson, Dennis Hahn, Max Miceli, Russ Jarman Price, Mike

Randall, Cody Simmonds, Paul Simón, Katy Wignall, Lindsay Wolff Logsdon, and Snow Zhou. They helped me polish the agile-strategy formula until it shone like a new Tesla roadster.

I was thrilled to get insightful comments and practical help from a number of authors I respect. These include Niraj Dawar, Kevin Duncan, Robert Jones, John Spence, Paco Underhill, and Dr. Kit Yarrow. You can find their books on Amazon; they're all essential reading.

I'd also like to thank a few other authors who've influenced my thinking on brand strategy: David Aaker, Clayton Christensen, Peter F. Drucker, Seth Godin, Gary Hamel, Roger L. Martin, Tom Peters, Al Ries, and Michael Schrage.

Thanks also to my inner circle of family and friends, especially Nancy Dillon, Peter Girolamo, and my brother Peter Neumeier, who gave me honest critiques and wonderfully detailed suggestions.

My heartfelt gratitude goes to colleagues and followers who participated in a marathon town-hall discussion of an early draft. This group of readers from around the world devoted up to six hours of their valuable time to answer questions and debate the book's merits on LinkedIn. Especially helpful were Wijnand Baretta, Zack Chmeis, Germund Daal, Matt Davies, Harry Elonen, Rudolf Greger, Kris Hans, Greg Hansen, Brandon Hoe, Nejdeh Hovanessian, Nick Jackson, Kirsten Jarvi, Michael Jones, Robin Melina Kinsman, Lulu Raghavan, Nigel Reyes, Todd Shaw, Lloyd Sigler, Slava, Patrick Troppe, and Ahmad Vaseem.

Others who offered feedback were Ben Acquaye, Leonardo Augó, Ben Barclay, David Beston, Michael Burnett, Ben Burns, Ayse Birsel, Brendan Bolt, Laurent Bouty, David Allan Chin, Shota Chinchaladaze, Chad Coleman, Franci Cronje, Thomas Cutler, Micah Eberman, Charles Erdman, Ken Feather, Sofia Frisk, Luis E. Garcia, Gregory Gornik, Peter Gwen, Kris Hans, Tijl Hoornstra, Edward Johansson, Lauri Jutila, Josh Levine,

Thanks

Dustin Ljung, Chris Martin, Pat McMahon, Richard McMurray, Carme Mont, Jill Neely, Leon Odey-Knight, Nur Partridge, Stephan Riess, Steven Stark, Nick Steadman, Nico ten Hoor, Seth Taylor, David Townson, Gellan Watt, Aaron White, and Lars Winking. Thanks to all of you.

On the production side, I'd like to thank Zach Gajewski for copy editing, Jameson Spence for page design, and Happenstance for ebook programming.

Most of all, I'd like to thank my wife, Eileen, for supporting me through this endeavor and many others. She's not only the love of my life, but my closest reader, my most scrupulous editor, and my best friend.

THE AUTHOR

Marty Neumeier started his career as a designer, later adding writing and publishing to his list of credits. He has written eight books on brand, strategy, innovation, and company culture.

His first book, *The Brand Gap*, was conceived as a "whiteboard overview"—a highly visual book designed to be read on a short plane flight. It became an instant bestseller, hitting the top ten on Amazon in the first month. An online version has been viewed over 22 million times since then.

A second whiteboard overview, *Zag*, was named one of the "top 100 business books of all time." He quickly followed *Zag* with three books on design thinking: *The Designful Company*, *Metaskills*, and *The 46 Rules of Genius*.

During his five-decade career, he has worked closely with innovative companies such as Apple, Sun Microsystems, Adobe, HP, Microsoft, Netscape, and Google, helping them to advance their brands and cultures.

Today he serves as Director of CEO Branding for Liquid Agency, a Silicon Valley firm that designs branded cultures for large organizations. He travels extensively as a workshop leader and speaker on the topics of brand, innovation, and leadership. When he's not traveling, he and his wife divide their time between California and southwest France. Connect with Marty on LinkedIn or subscribe to martyneumeier.com

Made in the USA
Middletown, DE
13 August 2022